T0319111

Contextual Innovation Management

Innovation has a pivotal role for companies in attaining business survival but making an organization innovative is not straightforward. By determining contextual factors, managers can help decide how to employ a portfolio of innovation management processes.

This book explores how contingency influence the management of innovation. Taking the perspective of innovation managers, the authors focus on the decision-making process to demonstrate that different approaches are required depending on the business context. In breaking the process into three levels (culture, industry and company), the book helps choose an optimal innovative approach.

With references to real-world innovation cases and organizations, this book will prove useful reading for students and researchers in the field of innovation studies and management.

Patrick van der Duin is Managing Director of the Netherlands Study Centre for Technology Trends.

Roland Ortt is Associate Professor of Technology and Innovation Management at Delft University of Technology, the Netherlands.

Routledge Studies in Innovation, Organizations
and Technology

For more information about this series, please visit www.routledge.
com/Routledge-Studies-in-Innovation-Organizations-and-Technology/
book-series/RIOT

Contextual Innovation Management

Adapting Innovation Processes to Different Situations

Patrick van der Duin and Roland Ortt

Routledge
Taylor & Francis Group

LONDON AND NEW YORK

First published 2020 by Routledge

2 Park Square, Milton Park, Abingdon, Oxon OX14 4RN
605 Third Avenue, New York, NY 10017

Routledge is an imprint of the Taylor & Francis Group, an informa business

First issued in paperback 2021

Library of Congress Cataloging-in-Publication Data
A catalog record for this book has been requested

ISBN: 978-1-138-92031-6 (hbk)
ISBN: 978-1-03-217428-0 (pbk)
DOI: 10.4324/9781315687131

Typeset in Sabon
by Apex CoVantage, LLC

In loving memory of Theo van der Duin

In loving memory of Henk Ortt

Contents

Figures, Tables, and Boxes

Figures

Tables

Boxes

Preface

Although every book has a clear beginning (and end), it is more difficult to indicate when the thinking about this book began. If we attempted to estimate when we started to think about this book, it would have been somewhere in the period that we published an article in the *European Journal of Innovation Management*[1] about different generations of innovation management. Although this historic layout looked very charming and therefore very convincing, we did not fully trust this stylized layout. It did not match the wide variety of innovation management practices that we encountered in the literature and that we could remember from the time we were both employed at KPN Research and engaged in innovation in a daily and practical manner. So many companies, in so many sectors, with so many different visions and missions, and with such different sizes and activities, they cannot and should not all be grouped together and not be summarized in a generation. The desire to get a clear overview of different practices of innovation is naturally justified. In fact, it is the task of science to provide structure to our unruly reality, to provide the necessary abstraction and to focus on the essences, in short: to show the forest through the trees. But then it must be the right abstractions, essences, and trees.

The naming of variety is necessary but not sufficient to understand and explain how organizations innovate. There must be a clear and workable middle ground between the indiscriminate acceptance of variety and the excessive styling of the different ways in which organizations manage their innovation processes. In this book, we propose to take this middle course by starting from the contingency approach whereby organizations are supposed to adapt their way of operating to the demands made on them by their environment (context). However, we have not opted for a "pure" interpretation and application of the contingency theory, but for a milder variant, which in turn is also a middle ground. Namely, that between contingency theory and universalism, where the last variant starts from the view that there really should only be one way in which companies operate if they want to be successful. We have therefore opted for a contextual approach whereby organizations adapt to their environment, but in which we do apply a certain degree of clustering. This clustering consists of effective combinations between the contextual factors that are part of the context of the organization and the different ways of innovating. Effectiveness then relates to the positive influence that the contextual approach to innovation has on the innovative capacity of the organization in particular and the performance of the organization in general.

In this book, the contextual approach to innovation management builds up by first criticizing thinking and acting in terms of success factors. Success factors implicitly assume a kind of generalism that we think does not hold. From there, it is possible to systematically look at potentially relevant contextual factors. By combining these with the different ways of innovating, as the modern history of innovation shows, we create a theoretical framework that enables organizations to innovate contextually. The cases in this book show what this application can look like in practice by linking it to addressing specific innovation problems of organizations. For a correct and permanent application of contextual innovation management, it is important to monitor how it works and to ensure that it is clear to innovation managers how this approach can be implemented in organizations, how it can be ensured organizationally and which organizational conditions should be met to enable the contextual approach to innovation management.

As we said, it is difficult to indicate when a book starts and when a book ends. As far as we are concerned, this book does not end and the theory of contextual innovation management will continue to be a living theory that will be applied by many organizations and will continue to feed the thinking about this theory. Only in this way will the management of innovation processes be permanently innovated.

Patrick van der Duin and Roland Ortt
January 2020

Note

1 Ortt, J.R. and P.A. van der Duin (2008). The evolution of innovation management towards contextual innovation. *European Journal of Innovation Management*, Vol.11, No.4, pp. 522–538

Acknowledgements

We want to thank Wieger Aarts, Geert de Jong, Edwin Oudijn, and Mirjam Fuchs for their comprehensive contribution to Chapter 6. Many thanks also to Japke Schreuders of the Netherlands Study Centre for Technology Trends for editing the text and to Yolanda Vredeveld of Delft University of Technology for making the figures and tables. And of course thanks to Mary del Plato from the Taylor & Francis Group for her endless patience. . . .

1 Generations of Innovation Management

Innovations have changed our society and society has shaped innovations in an evolutionary process. And just as society and innovations have changed each other, the practice of innovation, i.e., the innovation process, has also changed considerably. In a simplification one could recognize four separate generations in innovation management after the Second World War: 1) technology/science push; 2) market pull; 3) combination of science/technology push and market pull; and 4) networked innovation. This change of the innovation process is indeed evolutionary: each generation is both a general improvement of the previous generation and an adaptation to the changing societal and economic context.

The four subsequent generations indicate the vision that a dominant kind of innovation process can be distinguished in each period. But we think that this vision does not hold; different approaches to innovation management have always coexisted. Even if there would be a dominant approach to innovation, innovative organizations or networks of innovative organizations design the innovation process that fits their context. Sometimes an approach to innovation is adopted that resembles the dominant approach in the first generation, sometimes an approach of one of the later generations is adopted. This statement implies that it is of paramount importance to know the relevant factors in the context, and how they relate to the choice to design a particular innovation process.

1.1 Introduction

Human beings have always created new tools, technologies, products, and services. They have designed and implemented new working processes and production processes and envisioned new types of organizations. Innovations have pervaded society and conversely, have been shaped by society. The way we organize or manage innovation processes has also evolved over time. To put it differently: we have innovated the innovation process over time. Indeed, philosopher Alfred Whitehead once said that the greatest invention of 19th century was the invention of the method of invention, to which Burns and Stalker add that the 20th century was "to organize inventiveness" (1961, p. 22). Perhaps the 21st century will be about organizing, managing, or innovating the innovation process. This chapter provides an overview of the changes in innovation management in large companies during the last seventy years. We will distinguish four different generations in innovation management.

Different terms are used to indicate our focus of attention: generations of subsequent innovation processes (e.g., Rothwell, 1994), new product development processes (e.g., Cooper, 1994; Page, 1994; Griffin, 1997), innovation management approaches (e.g., Miller, 2001) and R&D management approaches (e.g., Niosi, 1999; Liyanage et al., 1999). Before moving on, we briefly define the relevant terms to indicate their relationship.

An *invention* is an idea that can be demonstrated in a prototype or as a working principle and an *innovation* is defined as a new product, service, or process that can be marketed or implemented (Utterback and Brown, 1972; Weiss and Birnbaum, 1989). An invention can be turned into an innovation when the prototype or working principle is turned into a new product, service or process. Here we consider an innovation as "new-to-the-company" because this type of newness requires an innovation process. The time between the invention and the first introduction of an innovation based on this invention can last long, much longer than the time required for a single innovation process (Ortt, 2010). In practice different organizations tend to develop similar innovations and hence various parallel innovation processes may shape the overall innovation process. Furthermore, it is shown that after an invention, the development of an innovation may be delayed or postponed for various reasons such as a lack of funding or no sense of urgency to develop the innovation (Van de Ven et al., 2008; Markham et al., 2010).

An innovation process describes the various stages in which an innovation is developed and the main activities that are performed at each stage. Invention processes are often different from innovation processes in that inventions can be serendipitous (Halacy, 1967; Van Andel, 1992) and invention processes are therefore less easy to plan than innovation processes. Innovation management refers to the governance and organization of the innovation process. Although the meaning of R&D management and that of innovation management to some extent overlap, that does not mean they are interchangeable. On the one hand, R&D management can be considered a broader term than innovation management, since it contains invention as well as innovation processes. On the other hand, R&D management usually focuses on a specific approach to innovation management in large companies and as such innovation management can be considered the broader of the two terms.

1.2 Finding Generations of Innovation Management

Innovation management has changed over time and it appears that every timeframe has its own notions of what successful or best practices are. We provide a historical account of the development of innovation management after WOII by describing four generations of innovation management and their organizational and societal context, including the advantages and disadvantages of the various generations. These so-called innovation management generations are descriptions "of what constitutes the dominant model of best practice" (Rothwell, 1994, p. 23). We carried out four steps: 1) Finding sources that describe generations of innovation management; 2) comparing the number of generations; 3) comparing the timing of the generations; 4) choosing the aspects that will be described for each generation.

Finding Sources

The main developments in innovation management are discussed in various areas of scientific literature. First, they are discussed in the literature about trends and developments in innovation (e.g. Gupta and Wilemon, 1996; Ortt and Smits, 2006; Smits and Kuhlmann, 2004; Wind and Mahajan, 1997). Second, they are assessed in large-scale empirical research projects focusing on new product development practices (e.g. Page, 1994; Griffin, 1997). Third, they are discussed in the literature about R&D and innovation management generations (e.g. Amidon Rogers, 1996; Cooper, 1994; Liyanage et al., 1999; Miller, 2001; Niosi, 1999; Rothwell, 1994; Roussel et al., 1991).

Comparing the Number of Generations

In the literature on generations, different authors have identified different numbers of generations. Both Rothwell (1994) and Amidon Rogers (1996) distinguish five generations, Yakhlef (2005) six generations, whereas Miller (2001), Liyanage et al. (1999), and Niosi (1999) identify four generations, and Cooper (1994) three. In this chapter, we use a framework of four generations, because we believe that the alleged "fifth and sixth generations" are merely an implementation of the fourth generation, a view that Rothwell (1994), one of the authors distinguishing a fifth generation, shares: "The development of 5G is essentially a development of the 4G (parallel, integrated) process" (Rothwell, 1994).

Comparing the Timing of Generations

There is also variation with regard to the timing of the various generations, in some cases more than a decade. Miller (2001), for example, places the second generation between 1950 and 1985, whereas Niosi (1999) places the same generation between the early 1960s and the early 1970s. Although it is not always clear how the various authors arrived at their verdict, the main idea is to indicate when a specific innovation management approach was considered to be the dominant (i.e., most commonly applied) best practice model. We adopt a different procedure by using hallmarks in the societal context to establish when a specific generation prevailed. Thus, we place the first generation between the end of the Second World War and the mid-1960s (see also: Godin, 2006). In the mid-1960s, a broad awareness emerged about the potentially negative societal effects of technology (Hughes, 1975). We place the second generation between the mid-1960s and the late 1970s. The late 1970s saw a recession that had a major impact on the resources that were allocated by companies and governmental organizations to innovation. We place the third generation between the late 1970s and the early 1990s, at which point the Internet made its commercial presence felt. The Internet has played a crucial role in people's and organizations' ability to cooperate at a distance and it has further stimulated the emergence of a truly global economy. The fourth generation started in the early 1990s and it was the dominant approach for more than a decade. However, nowadays we think different approaches are adopted next to each other, depending on the requirements of the context. We believe that the emergence of ever-newer generations of dominant innovation management approaches has come to an end.

Choosing the Aspects to Describe Generations

For each of the generations we focus on different aspects. We look at the structure and organization of the innovation process as a project, we track the structure of the typical organization within which the process was organized, and we summarize some of the main market and societal developments with an impact on companies in general and their innovation process in particular.

1.3 The Generations of Innovation Management

With the emergence of the first R&D departments in the late 19th century, innovation in large companies changed. These departments were based on the notion that scientific research was an important prerequisite for successful innovation. As a result, some of the large companies integrated basic research, applied research, and development efforts (Bassala, 2001; Niosi, 1999; Chiesa, 2001). Later many companies outsourced their basic research activities to universities or specialized research companies. Although the applied research activities and development efforts have remained an important element in innovation, they have become more separated in many companies. Research usually has remained a central corporate activity and development is re-allocated to different business units (Chiesa, 2001). But, that division is based on a separation between deliberate research and invention activities on the one hand and development and innovation activities on the other hand, a division that does not take inventions into account that appear while working on development of innovation or while solving practical issues. Rosenberg (1982), for example, shows how many fundamental inventions and basic research notions appeared while solving practical issues.

Niosi (1999, p. 117) provides a concise description of the successive generations reflecting the evolution of innovation management from the 1950s:

> The first generation brought the corporate R&D laboratory. The second generation adapted project management methods to R&D. The third brought internal collaboration between different functions in the firm. The fourth adds routines designed to make more flexible the conduct of the R&D function through the incorporation of the knowledge of users and competitors.

The First Generation

From the late 19th century up to the mid-1960s, social attitudes toward scientific advance and technological innovation were generally favorable. Achievements in science and technology were thought to reflect the power of the countries and were displayed from the 19th century on, at World Exhibitions.

Inventors were worshipped like heroes (Noble, 1980). Technological developments were primarily driven by scientific progress, and they were expected to solve society's main problems (Rothwell, 1994; Roussel et al., 1991). After the Second World War, governments stimulated technological innovation, very much inspired by Vannevar Bush's publication *Science: The endless frontier* (1945) (Godin, 2006). From the Second World War until 1985, the US government, for example, spent more money on R&D than the complete US industrial sector (Chesbrough, 2003). Governments did so for a number of reasons. First, technological innovation was needed for military purposes. The Cold War demanded technological leadership. Second, technological innovation formed the heart of new and renewed industries (Ortt and Smits, 2006). Partly as a result of technological progress, economic conditions flourished after the Second World War. Consumer demand exceeded supply. These social developments were reflected in the strategy and structure of organizations. Companies were often technology oriented; they focused on innovation and growth and they usually adopted a functional structure.

The societal and organizational context had a direct effect on the ideas about innovation management. Innovation was primarily seen as science and technology driven. In fact, the corporate R&D-labs were based on the notion that invention and innovation processes had to be integrated. These labs were organized like traditional universities, in mono-disciplinary departments (Roussel et al., 1991). They were regarded as large staff departments tied to and funded by the headquarters of organizations to grant them the freedom that was thought to be necessary to develop breakthrough technologies. In general, the structure of innovation processes was linear-sequential and of a technology push nature. In the course of the innovation process, an innovation was managed by various departments that each contributed to the end product. An effect of the fact that demand exceeded supply in many markets was that innovation management could focus on technology rather than on market needs. Both the generous government funding (for industry and military purposes) and corporate growth allowed companies to focus on the kind of long-term research that was required for technological breakthroughs. Although this generation may seem outdated now, it is important to notice that the ideas on corporate research emerged already in the late 19th century. Typical corporate labs that emerged early on were the Bell labs and the corporate labs from General Electric, and from Dupont. These corporate labs invented some of the radically new breakthrough technologies that have shaped our current society such as the transistor, solar cells, integrated circuits, mobile telephony, ECG, nylon, and Kevlar.

Compared to earlier ideas about innovation management, the first generation of innovation management had several advantages, such as scientific freedom and large budgets for researchers and developers and the development of many radical innovations. Although science-based corporate labs such as the Bell labs and the lab from General Electric indeed yielded many breakthrough technologies (Buderi, 2000; Chesbrough, 2003), in hindsight their approach also had significant disadvantages. Because an innovation would tend to move from department to department, and project management had yet to be introduced, it was not always clear who was responsible. This also implies that little attention was paid to the overall transformation process from idea to innovation. Scientific freedom of professionals seemed more important than commercial relevance for the company. Subsequently, innovation processes sometimes lacked a strategic goal. Market needs and commercial aspects were incorporated late in the process, as a result of which commercial failures were discovered relatively late and too much effort was put into unsuccessful innovation processes.

The Second Generation

Increased public awareness of the ethical, social, and environmental consequences of business decisions can be noticed from the mid-1960s on (Gupta and Wilemon, 1996; Wind and Mahajan, 1997).

> College students of the late sixties and early seventies know well—even contributed to—the sharp reaction against American technology.

This attitude was and is interesting in itself, but the interest is heightened for an older generation that recalls the enthusiastic commitment to technology that was widespread only decades ago.

(Hughes, 1975, p. vii)

Rothwell (1994) summarizes how the market conditions changed in the wake of these societal developments. Although it is a period of relative prosperity, the economic growth that characterized the post-war period slowed down after the mid-1960s. Demand roughly equaled supply. From the mid-1960s onwards attention in society focused on the demand side of the market. Competition intensified because the growth targets of companies could no longer be achieved on the basis of the intrinsic growth of the market. Consequently, company strategies focused on growth and diversification to attain economies of scale and to reduce financial risks. Corporations developed divisional structures to meet the requirements of their diversified companies. Channon (1973) shows, for example, that in the UK, from 1960 to 1970, significant changes took place in the mainstream organizational structures. In 1960, 24% of the manufacturing companies in the UK had a functional organization structure against 33% with a multi-divisional structure. In 1970, these figures were 8% and 71% respectively. In a single decade, the multi-divisional organizational structure had become widely accepted.

In this context the innovation management approach had to change. First, due to the new market conditions (supply equaled demand and an increased awareness of ethical, social, and environmental issues) consumer aspects had to be taken into account earlier in the innovation process (Levitt, 1960; Sissors, 1966; Day, 1981). Consumer research rather than scientific research became the basis for new product ideas (Fornell and Menko, 1981). As a result, the interface between R&D and marketing became more important (Souder, 1988). Second, the scientific freedom and the accompanying lack of direct market results that characterized the previous generation were considered unacceptable in this situation with increased competition. Divisions started funding R&D, became internal clients and therefore demanded that R&D efforts be more closely related to their business (Corcoran, 1994; Gupta and Wilemon, 1996). The focus on market results and efficiency also required a stricter governance of innovation processes. A project management approach was adopted and a project leader, rather than subsequent managers of departments, was given final responsibility. Third, research and development were separated because divisions were funding applied development efforts while corporate headquarters continued to fund basic research. Fourth, both the consumer orientation and the influence of divisions called for multidisciplinary cooperation in innovation processes (Liyanage et al., 1999). The multidisciplinary projects stimulated R&D institutes to abandon the functional structure and to adopt a matrix-based organizational structure in which disciplines formed one and specific purposes or customers formed another axis of the matrix. The innovation process remained essentially linear-sequential, albeit of a market pull nature.

In light of the context, the second-generation approach of innovation management had many advantages. the market orientation reduced the risk associated with innovation and, together with the adoption of a project management approach, reduced the time-to-market of innovation processes. With hindsight, however, we see that the consumer-oriented approach that prevailed between the mid-1960s and the late 1970s was not perfect either, because potential consumers were not able to express their needs beyond those solved by familiar products (Bennett and Cooper, 1982; Tauber, 1974). As a result there was a focus on small improvements of existing products rather than on more radical innovations (Bennett and Cooper, 1982; Corcoran, 1994; Szakonyi, 1998). Another drawback of the second generation was that innovation projects were treated separately. As each project served the goals of different internal company clients, relationships amongst the innovation projects/processes and the strategic goals of the company were hardly established.

The Third Generation

The period between the late 1970s and the early 1990s was a period of economic decline because of two oil crises, inflation, and demand saturation in Europe and the United States. Supply exceeded demand, unemployment figures rose and resource constraints (especially regarding oil and oil-based products) had an important effect on the market. Companies started to focus on controlling and reducing costs rather than on realizing growth (Rothwell, 1994). The hierarchically organized companies were transformed into more flexible companies, for example by forming relatively independent business units.

In this societal and organizational context, innovation was increasingly seen as an investment that should make a relevant contribution to the business units' strategies (Roussel et al., 1991). Innovation processes were also organized in programs, to form a balanced portfolio of processes aimed at strengthening the strategic goals of these business units. Empirical studies indicate that technology push and need pull models of innovation were extreme and atypical examples of a more general process of interaction between technological capabilities and market needs (Mowery and Rosenburg, 1979). The structure of innovation processes remained essentially linear, but with feedback loops and constant interaction with market-related and technological factors (Rothwell, 1994). The concept of Quality Function Deployment, proposed by Hauser and Clausing (1988) is an example of an approach that combined technology and market knowledge. Companies adopting third generation approaches tried to find partners with essential technological and market knowledge, and together they formed communication and innovation networks.

The third generation of innovation management combined the strong points and remedied the weak points of the two previous generations. The main disadvantage of the third generation was a sole focus on the (end) product that was the outcome of the innovation process rather than the organizational and market changes that were required to introduce this product successfully in the market (Miller, 2001). Traditionally, R&D labs had no experience with organizational and market-related renewal, which used to be the domains of top managers and marketeers respectively. Involvement of top managers in R&D and close links between innovation processes and strategic company goals were important, since they facilitated the transfer of innovations from the R&D labs to the parent company.

The Fourth Generation

Between the early 1990s and the early 2000s, technological developments in communication and information technology stimulated a further globalization. Both globalization and the changes in communication and information technology influenced the organization and management of design, manufacturing, distribution, and marketing processes. Globalization forced companies to focus on their core competences (Prahalad and Hamel, 1994), and it has further increased the level of competition both in domestic and global markets (Gupta and Wilemon, 1996). Another consequence of the advances in technology was that the knowledge required to develop new products evolved. Tidd et al. (2001), for example, showed that the number of technologies required to develop and produce mobile phones grew considerably in a few years. In many cases, technological competences to develop new products have become too complex to be mastered by a single company.

As a result of the developments just outlined, during the fourth generation both invention and innovation processes increasingly involved the management of international alliances (Hagedoorn and Schakenraad, 1990). Gassmann and Von Zedtwitz (1999a) indicated that, for example, from 1986 onwards Swiss and Dutch companies had more labs abroad than at home because of the relatively small sizes of their domestic markets and a lack of R&D resources in their own country. Between the early 1990s and the start of the 21st century innovation projects were no longer carried out in the isolation of R&D departments, but instead were embedded in large networks with internal (other company departments) and external partners (universities, suppliers, customers, etc.). More specifically, the degree of integration of innovating companies with their suppliers and customers increased (Scott, 2001). In many markets, suppliers had become more capable and therefore participated as partners in innovation processes rather than merely served as producers of pre-specified parts (Chesbrough, 2003). Developments in communication and information technology facilitated intra- and inter-organizational cooperation in innovation processes (Howells, 1990). Exploitation has always been a bottleneck in innovation. The fourth generation paid more attention to market-related and organizational changes required to successfully introduce and implement product innovations in the market. The term innovation extended beyond product innovation to include process, organizational, and market-related innovation (Trott, 2002), and business development becomes an integral part of innovation management (Chesbrough, 2003).

A disadvantage of the fourth generation of innovation management was its complexity. To handle this complexity, more flexible organizations and the application of information technology were proposed.

The fourth generation of innovation management can be characterized by openness, meaning that a network of partners jointly innovates so innovation efforts were distributed while customers were involved as co-innovators (Baldwin and Von Hippel, 2011). Innovation entailed more than technology and products: it started to include the entire marketing mix, complementary products and services, business models, and innovative production approaches, for example. The subsequent generations of innovation management are summarized in Table 1.1.

1.4 From Generations to Coexisting Approaches of Innovation Management

As we described in section 1.1., generations of innovation management can be perceived as 'dominant models of best practice'. Next to each dominant practice or approach, however, other approaches can be applied. Indeed, in practice multiple approaches always have been applied in parallel. Presently, we observe a large variety in innovation management approaches, and hence a dominant approach can no longer be distinguished. The range of historical generations has come to an end[1] and instead a kind of postmodern approach to innovation management has emerged. That is, different approaches of innovation management coexist and form a kind of mosaic although, unlike postmodern thinking, this mosaic of practices is not without structure. Organizations do deliberately choose particular approaches, and for good reasons, as we will see in the following chapters.

The main question of this book is: how do organizations choose a particular innovation management approach? What is the current mosaic of approaches and which factors determine or guide a choice between them? We will claim that there is no longer a dominant approach or best practice; the choice for a particular approach depends on the context of an organization. We refer to this notion as *contextual innovation management*.

Table 1.1 An Overview of Subsequent Innovation Management Approaches, Their Context and Their (Dis)Advantages.

Period	Societal and organizational context of innovation	Innovation approach	Disadvantages of the approach
From the post-war period to the mid-1960s	**Society** Society has a generally favourable attitude toward scientific progress. Governments subsidize R&D in universities and companies to stimulate economic growth and to attain military leadership. Consumer demand exceeds the supply of goods. **Organizations** Organizational strategies are generally technology-oriented and focus on innovation and growth. Most organizations are functionally organized.	**Technology (science) push:** The process of commercialization of technological change is generally perceived as a linear progression from scientific discovery to the marketplace. Many R&D-departments are staff departments that are structured like scientific institutions. **Structure innovation process** Linear-sequential process from department to department, starting with scientific discovery.	**Disadvantages** Little attention is paid to the entire process or the role of the marketplace. Scientific freedom is more important than business results. Innovation projects serve no strategic goals. Commercial aspects are incorporated late. Professional project management practices are not applied.
From the mid-1960s to the late 1970s	**Society** This is a period of relative prosperity, although economic growth slows down. Demand more or less equals supply. Many markets show an increase in competition. Government policies tend to emphasize demand-side factors. **Organizations** Organization strategies generally focus on growth, to attain economies of scale; and on diversification, to reduce financial risks. Many organizations adopt a multi-divisional structure.	**Market pull (need-pull):** Technological change is rationalized, needs are considered more important to innovation than scientific and technological progress. Because innovation processes are managed as projects, R&D institutes are organized in a matrix. Divisions become internal clients that directly fund R&D. **Structure innovation process** Innovation is generally organized in multidisciplinary projects. Linear-sequential process in a project, starting with market need.	**Disadvantages** Neglects long-term innovation programs and therefore leads to 'incrementalism'. Focuses on evolutionary improvements rather than breakthroughs. Projects are individual units; strategic relationships between these projects and corporate goals are not established.

(Continued)

Table 1.1 (Continued)

Period	Societal and organizational context of innovation	Innovation approach	Disadvantages of the approach
From the late 1970s to the early 1990s	**Society** This is a period with two oil crises, inflation, and demand saturation. Supply exceeds demand, unemployment figures rise. **Organizations** Company strategies generally focus on cost control and reduction. Organizations become more flexible and less hierarchically organized. Responsibilities are delegated to business units.	**Market pull and technology push combined:** Knowledge about technology and market needs is used throughout the innovation process. To obtain this knowledge (communication) networks are formed with internal and external partners. Innovation projects become part of a portfolio of projects aligned with the corporate strategy. **Structure innovation process** Model of an essentially sequential process with feedback loops and interaction with market needs and state-of-the-art technology.	**Disadvantages** Focuses on product and process innovations rather than market and organizational innovations. Focuses on the creation of innovations rather than the exploitation.
From the early 1990s to the early 2000s	**Society** Globalization is important in this period, international competition increases. Organizations realize the strategic importance of technologies. Information and communication technologies influence internal and external business processes. **Organizations** Company strategies generally concentrate on core competences. Strategic alliances and external networking become important. Time-to-market becomes more important. More organizations adopt team-based and project-based structures.	**Innovation in alliances; parallel and integrated innovation, from innovation to new business development (NBD):** Innovation management means managing research links and external research environments. Parallel processes are used to involve multiple actors and to increase the development speed. The fourth generation includes business and market models. **Structure innovation process** Coordinated process of innovation in a network of partners. The required coordination is often attained by system integration (with key suppliers and customers) and parallel development (of components or modules of the innovation).	**Possibilities for improvement** Increased networking and integration with internal and external partners. Increased use of information technology to cooperate and communicate. Increased flexibility of the structure of innovation processes.

Source: The overview of four innovation management approaches is based on the following sources: Liyanage et al., 1999; Miller, 2001; Niosi, 1999; Rothwell, 1994; Roussel et al., 1991.

In line with the development of generations of innovation management we see that contextual innovation management is driven by the goal to obtain increased levels of effectiveness and efficiency in innovation and by the notion that innovation approaches need to be adapted to the context. However, the notion of one overarching societal context does no longer hold and as a result the idea of one dominant approach to innovation management is no longer valid. Previous approaches may, in specific contexts, represent a good way to manage innovation and hence generations of innovation management are not seen as fully outdated but instead components of these approaches are still considered when adapting the innovation approach to various contexts. The increasing variety in approaches renders the choice of a particular approach more difficult than ever but at the same time more interesting and relevant.

Box 1.1   Open Innovation Is Not New

One of the most important notions in innovation management during the last two decades is the 'open innovation' paradigm developed by Henry Chesbrough in 2003 in his book *Open innovation. The new imperative for creating and profiting from new technology.* In this book, Chesbrough describes how companies should open their innovation processes and start working together by sharing their knowledge and by paying more attention to the business model of the innovation that is under development. After this book, many companies adopted this approach as their dominant approach to innovation and many innovation scholars used this theory as a basis for their scientific research.

However, was this a truly new approach to innovation? Paul Trott and Dap Hartmann wrote in 2009 an article with the pertinent title: 'Why 'open innovation' is old wine in new bottles'. They state that the open innovation paradigm is not new but that many of its principles already were applied by companies decades before Chesbrough put that in his theory. Also, they 'accuse' Chesbrough in putting forward his concept by using a 'straw man argument'; he gives a faulty description of 'closed innovation' and thereby gives 'his' open innovation a better and much modern connotation.

The increased diversity of innovation management approaches is rooted in the mechanisms of adaptation and improvement. Organizational environments change faster and hence organizations become (or need to become) more dynamic and more connected to each other. Organizations from different industries join forces and increasingly combine their technologies and products. Groups of organizations promote platforms that allow a range of cross-innovations. An example of the merging of different industries is provided by the telecommunication and computing market, both of which had remarkably different innovation management approaches prior to melting together. In the telecommunication industry, many nations allowed monopolies, and these monopolistic companies adopted an innovation approach in which telecommunication innovations were tested fully and standardized prior to introduction or implementation. In contrast, in the computing or IT industry, beta versions of innovations were already introduced in a niche of the market and then gradually improved and adapted using the feedback from the first users. It may come as no surprise that cooperation between companies from such different industries with such a different take on innovation approaches can be difficult (Berkhout and Van der Duin, 2007). Indeed, it can be argued that organizations that are able to adopt a variety of innovation approaches turn out to be more successful because they master the ability to adapt and combine them, which allows them to keep abreast of the changing context that sets different requirements to the innovation approach.

Box 1.2   Innovation Approaches at Shell

Oil (or energy) company Shell has a long history of innovation and is the ultimate example of that a company developing new products and services and also innovating itself as a company. The large size of the organization, the differences in markets is it serving, and the just-mentioned emphasis on innovation, has led to different approaches to innovation management. According to Verloop (2006), Shell as a company distinguishes between 'inside-the-box' and 'outside-the-box'-innovations. These approaches lead to different types of innovation models that are applied in different business units of Shell. For instance, they use:

- a (classical) 'Cascade model': supply-driven, sequential innovation
- a 'Bridge model': demand-driven, opportunistic innovation
- a 'TriPod model': 'change' driven, sustainable innovation

Box 1.3   Innovation Approaches at Philips

Dutch originating company Philips has a great record in innovation. Their R&D facility, the 'NatLab', was one of the worldwide famous R&D facilities of large multinationals responsible for many great scientific inventions and innovations. The NatLab turned itself in the 2000s into the 'High-Tech Campus', one of the first large innovation centers based on the 'open innovation' principle. In an article in 2006, Van den Elst, Tol, and Smits gave an overview of Philips' different approaches to innovation at that time. They distinguish between seven different innovation approaches:

- Lead-customer–driven innovation in a business-to-business context;
- Consumer-driven innovation in consumer markets;
- Innovation in functionally specialized environments;
- Innovation based on scientific research;
- Innovation in the context of business alliances;
- Innovation through the Philips technology business incubator;
- Innovation through corporate venturing.

The most important criterion to decide upon which innovation approach to follow is the specific business context (market) of the business unit. Although this stimulates the effectiveness of their innovation processes, a problem occurs when different business units are innovating together because their different innovation approaches collide with each other.

1.5 Concluding Remarks

In this chapter, four innovation management generations were discussed, representing the mainstream ideas about innovation management after the Second World War. We have compared the development of innovation management to an evolution, a biological metaphor. In a similar vein, this metaphor is also used by other authors to describe the history of technology and to explain the evolution of technological artefacts (e.g., Bassala, 2001). Evolution (of organisms or technological artefacts) not only refers to gradual change, it also refers to growing diversity and subsequent selection. The term 'Darwinian process' refers to the principle of survival of the fittest. We state that the evolution of innovation management is driven by the combined effect of trying to overcome the (dis)advantages of earlier approaches in the same context and of adapting the approaches to a changing context.

Innovation can be considered as a multi-level and complex phenomenon. The developments in society, in the industrial environment, in the way companies are organized and structured, and in the way innovation processes are organized and structured as projects, seem to be interrelated. The influence goes both ways: from the environment to the innovation management approach and the other way around. New generations of innovation management emerged because of the adaptation of innovation management to a changing environment. An example is provided by the shift from an overall excess in demand during the post-war period until the mid-1960s to a balance between demand and supply from the 1960s on and an excess in supply from the late 1970s on. This change in the macro-environment undoubtedly had an effect on the shift from a mainly technology-centered innovation management approach to a more consumer-oriented innovation management approach.

New generations of innovation management also emerged when improved practices to manage innovation processes were found. The shift from a linear-sequential approach in innovation management, where subsequent departments were involved to develop innovations, was improved into a more project-based approach in which a team of members coming from different departments were involved in the entire innovation process. This can be seen as a kind of general improvement that holds across a wide variety of contexts. This project-based approach, in turn, had an effect on the structure and organization of the companies. Employees were now working in cross-departmental projects when innovating. These types of working undoubtedly stimulated the formation of a matrix type of organizational structures in companies.

Note

1 Maybe comparable to Francis Fukuyama's famous notion of the 'end of history'.

2 Why Success Factors Are Not Successful

The historical development of innovation management shows that the method of innovation is changing. Innovation has become important for both companies and economies; being innovative has become synonymous with being successful. It is not without reason that a large amount of scientific and applied research is conducted into which factors explain the success of companies. After all, if one knows what those factors are, then it is only a matter of applying them and success is assured. Many of these types of research assume that there is one set of unchanging success factors that apply anywhere, anytime. But (unfortunately) that appears not to be the case. Indeed, investigations that lead to this have either not been properly carried out, or they result in factors that are so general that they are meaningless. Success factors that are always and everywhere valid simply do not exist. Often they only apply temporarily or in a local context. The successful management of a company or economy is therefore an extremely complex matter, whereby new success factors must be constantly sought for.

2.1 Introduction

Chapter 1 showed that there are different approaches to innovation management. However, many management scientists and consultants keep searching for a universal set of success factors for innovation. However, just as there is no such thing as a free lunch or a fast buck, there is no general recipe for obtaining success in business in general or innovation in particular. Such a recipe, if it would exist, is not only difficult to decipher but it would also constantly change. The road to success is not only long, but also full of obstacles and it often splits in different directions. Some might say that it is unfortunate that the formula for success is difficult to understand and even changes, because it makes business unnecessary complicated. However, in this book we claim that this should not be considered as a problem. Indeed, the change in successful business practices is an essential part of our capitalistic economic system and, more importantly, it is an essential condition that needs to be taken into account when managing companies. Ever-changing success formulas mean uncertainty for companies about what to do and what to decide and it is exactly this uncertainty that managers should embrace because it provides them with the required degrees of freedom to manage. Indeed, the essence of management is finding what works best for the organization and what does not. A business world with just one universal success formula would leave managers with no space to maneuver, no room to make their own decisions, no opportunity to distinguish themselves from other managers (and companies); in short, no room to excel.

A business world with a fixed success formula is a static one, devoid of change and innovation, a boring one, and (luckily) not a realistic one. Look around: change is everywhere, in technology, in society, in politics. And the way businesses should be managed would then stay the same? Why then should we be looking at and thinking about the world in the same way we have always done? In the words of economist and Nobel Prize-winner Douglass C. North: "If we are continually creating a new and novel world, how good is the theory that we have developed from past experiences to deal with this novel world?" (North, 2005, p. 13). Indeed, specifically with regard to innovation, Bessant et al. (2005) state that the prescriptive power of 'good practices' only works under conditions of stable markets but "is not a good guide when elements of discontinuity come into the equation" (p. 1366).

Nevertheless, many people, including scientists, managers, and business consultants, propagate the idea that business successes boil down to understanding and applying a few basic principles. Indeed, numerous studies on various management-related topics have been published on how to become successful. The huge diversity of success factors from these studies might give the proponents of the eternal and universal success formula a first clue that such a straightforward formula does not exist at all. The ongoing stream of such publications implies that such a simple formula is yet to be found. After all, why spend so many resources on studying how to become successful if a few principles would suffice?

Box 2.1   The Icarus Paradox: What Goes Up, Must Come Down

Success factors are not eternal but change over time. What works best in one period might give raise to failure in another period. A good illustration of this principle is the Icarus paradox as described by Danny Miller in his book *The Icarus Paradox* (1992b). According to Miller, the success of companies ends after a certain period because the same factor that has caused the success is subsequently responsible for its decline. Apparently, managers are not able to change their strategies but stick to original success formulas. More specifically, the success of companies lures them into failure through overconfidence, complacency, specialization, exaggeration, dogma, and ritual. Miller (1992b) states that: "(O)rganizations . . . extend their orientations until they reach dangerous extremes, their momentum issues in common trajectories of decline. And because successful types differ so much from one another, so will their trajectories". So, not only do organizations take different ways to success, so does their decline. The paradox is then that success can lead to failure because of these 'bad habits' and the causes of success are the same causes of failure (Miller, 1992b). Simply put: It is simply a case of "too much of a good thing" (idem, p. 31).

If we frame all this in our ideas about context and innovation, we consider the eagerness of managers to stick to their successful way of doing business is not in line with a dynamic business environment in which the successful way of doing business changes. The current successful practices are no longer in line with the current environmental demands and, of course, also of the future environment. "Never change a winning team" is a very likeable attitude but if managers "focus too much on protecting their current position at the expense of realizing what might be promising opportunities" (Amason and Mooney, 2008, p. 429) then failure might be the ultimate consequence. If you don't kill your darlings, to use another well-known expression, someone else will.

To conclude, recipes for success are not fixed. Due to changing environments, those same success factors and their underlying causes can turn into failure factors if managers do not pay sufficient attention to that changing environment and how that affects their business principles. For the (development of the) theory of contextual innovation management, it is important to note that the Icarus paradox does not only explain that business success is temporary and context-dependent, but also that the contextual bases for success factors will change over time. This leaves managers the challenging task to adjust their way of doing business on time: "it is important that we understand better how context biases managers as they identify opportunities and threats as they make strategic decisions" (Amason and Mooney, 2008, p. 429).

2.2 Searching for Success Factors

Looking for factors that explain why some organizations fail and others not is a very understandable ambition. Who would not like to know what works and what doesn't work? One can have different motives for this, ranging from a sincere interest in how business successes can be explained to a more practical motive to know those factors that enable someone to set up a successful business and to reap the financial profits from it. It would make the search and analysis of business success easier if there were a fixed set of explaining factors or guiding principles for business success.

There are many studies searching for success factors in management. The most popular ones do not concentrate so much on innovation success in particular but on overall business. Famous examples are *In search of excellence* by Peters and Waterman (1982) and *Built to Last— Successful habits of visionary companies* by Collins and Porras (1994). Often these types of studies are just as successful as tragic. They are the claim to fame for the authors involved but it doesn't take long before the limited added value of their studies become apparent, either because the data turns out to be wrong or because the examples that proved their point (i.e., successful companies) have in the meantime gone bankrupt or turned out to be unsuccessful in another way. This lack of sustainable success might be disappointing but given our standpoint on success factors (which we will develop during this chapter), for now we think that this disappointment is inevitable. With regard to innovation in particular, there are many studies aimed at finding the optimal way of innovating or, formulated the other way around, trying to explain why certain innovation processes fail (e.g., De Brentani, 1991; Damanpour, 1991; Cooper and Kleinschmidt, 1995; Griffin, 1997; Loewe et al., 2001; Burgers et al., 2008). For instance, Van der Panne et al. (2003), based on an extensive review of literature of determinants of success and failure of innovation, come to ten explaining factors such as firm culture, experience with innovation, and multidisciplinary R&D teams. These factors are rather concrete (although the question remains, for instance, what the 'firm culture' should be to support innovation)[1] but 'adequate timing of market introduction' and 'product quality and price relative to those of substitutes' are so general that are they are very difficult to falsify and therefore do not add to the investigation of how companies could and should innovate successfully. So, in addition to the temporal character of success factors, as shown by the fading added value of the studies by Peters and Waterman and by Collins and Porras, most success factors are formulated in such a general way that they become meaningless. After all, who would oppose innovations that have a high 'product quality and price ratio relative to those of substitutes?' (i.e., another success factor from the just mentioned study by Van der Panne et al. in 2003).

Nevertheless, they are too general for companies to put them in practice. Of course 'timing' (i.e., implementing innovations in the market at the right time) is important, but what is actually the right time or timing? Not surprisingly, in innovation management there is an ongoing debate about the right time to enter a market (see: Lieberman and Montgomery, 1998; Robinson and Min, 2002).

Another example of the rather general nature of success factors, which makes these hard to falsify and hence limits their scientific value, can also be found in a study by De Brentani (1991) into the development of new business services. Her study results in seventeen (independent) success factors and she concludes that 'descriptive dimensions' such as (the rather extensive)

> (R)esponding to market needs with new or changed services that offer clients both functional and experiential quality, that are innovative and truly superior to competitive offerings, and that fully benefit from a formal and well managed new service development process and from unique strengths and proficiencies of the firm are key requirements for creating and marketing winning new service products.
>
> (p. 56)

Doing well and even better than your competitors is the key to success. Who would oppose that? Then again, why would that add to our knowledge of innovation management?

Coming back to the point just made about the difficulty of implementing general success factors, note that we do not say that success factors should always be general. We only state that success factors are often defined as such to make sure that they are applicable and valid for a wide range of companies. However, the difficulty or impossibility of applying general success factors makes these factors even more tragic. After all, how tragic is it to know these factors and not being able to use them? It is like Cassandra's curse, being able to predict the future accurately and not being believed by a single soul. . . .

Another, very extensive study on success factors for 'new product development' is from Ernst (2002) who says that because innovation is important for companies, innovation managers are more than eager to know what these factors are. Many studies simply ask company managers, consultants, scientists, or other experts, what they perceive as success factors. In contrast, Ernst (2002) bases his list of success factors on empirical studies that aim at finding significant and empirically established relationships between relevant variables. He distinguishes between five categories: 1) NPD process, 2) organization, 3) culture, 4) role and commitment of senior management, and 5) strategy, each category having its own set of success factors. Ernst concludes that although many studies have 'an informant bias', "over a period of nearly thirty years, the results of empirical NPD research have remain constant" (p. 32). Although Ernst ascribes this to possible methodological flaws in the research, he also finds it conceivable that the findings of research have not been completely put into practice (idem.). One could argue that this says something about the gap between the scientific research into innovation management and the everyday practice of innovation management, but we put forward another reason, which is formulated by Ernst himself as follows: "situational influences on the success impact of individual variables in a contingency model are seldom incorporated in the empirical studies" (p. 33). 'Degree of newness', according to Ernst, might be such a contingency factor. We conclude that research into innovation (NPD) practices does not have sufficient eye for the differences in how organizations deal with innovation and that it is too much focused on generalizable results, which by nature will be rather constant over time and thereby difficult to apply.

Two other famous studies on success factors for innovation are the Project SAPPHO (Rothwell et al., 1974) and a study by Miller and Blais (1993) on modes of innovation in six industrial sectors (see the following). The SAPPHO-study "was designed as a systematic attempt to discover differences between successful and unsuccessful innovations" (p. 258). They found five *main areas* in which successful innovators distinguish themselves from companies who fail with regard to innovation (pp. 259–260):

1. A better understanding of user needs;
2. Paying more attention to marketing and publicity;
3. More efficient development (but not quicker);
4. More (specific) usage of outside technology and scientific advice;
5. Responsible individuals have more seniority and authority.

The SAPPHO-project was succeeded by project 'SAPPHO phase II' which was an extension with regard to the amount of companies investigated and basically confirmed the outcomes of the former project. Just as with the study by Van der Panne et al. (2003) the five success factors were very general. This leaves innovation managers once again with the huge task to operationalize these success factors since the attainment of the success factors should be implemented and their state be measured and monitored. Also the implementation of these success factors might become complicated because of the general nature. In particular, who would oppose implementing more efficient ways of developing new products? But the real question is of course what exactly is meant by efficient, and how to measure that precisely? In addition, is efficiency really such an important factor to judge the quality of an innovation process? And is this term not more suitable to judge more operational business processes like production, sales, and marketing?

This general nature of success factors found in various studies has two sides. The factors can be generalizable to companies or they can be generalizable to a period. The first side means that a certain success factor holds for every company without taking a specific period into account. The second side means that the found success factors are only relevant to a certain period but valid for each organization. The ultimate success factor would naturally be one that holds for every organization and in every period.

Some studies on success factors explicitly mention the context. Miller and Blais (1993) investigated the modes of innovation in six industrial sectors. They state that the actual modes of innovation of firms "are not only influenced by their formal strategies, but also by the industrial contexts in which they operate and by their specific organizational competencies" (p. 264). They consider these modes of innovation "as stable patterns of contextual strategic, structural and process variables serving as independent variables" (idem.). In particular they included the following contextual variables": rivalry in competition, uncertainty, and change in the environment, diversity/heterogeneity of the environment, globalization, and market structure. They come to the following *taxonomy* of modes of innovation: 1) science-based product innovators; 2) entrepreneurial fast-track experimenters; 3) global cost leaders; and 4) conventional reliance on IT and process adaptation.

This taxonomy resembles Pavitt's taxonomy of industries, each of which has a fundamentally different way to innovate (1984). Pavitt distinguishes three groups of industries: 1) the supplier dominated industries (such as the textile industry) where suppliers of machines drive innovation in the industry; 2) the production intensive industries (such as metal manufacture and automotive industries) that improve their own processes of production; and 3) science-based industries (such as the pharmaceutical industry) in which scientific institutes and efforts drive innovation.

Maffin et al. (1997) take into account both the company and project contexts which might explain that they do not use the term 'success factor' but 'best practice' (maybe 'good practice' was even a better term . . .). They conclude that "as a result of the complex and diverse nature of companies and their competitive environments, best practices for any one company is dependent on its own unique attributes" (p. 71).

Another study on factors that attempts to explain the success of innovation management is from Tidd and Thuriaux-Alemán (2016), who have investigated the 'innovation management practices' (IMPs) within and across various sectors. They find that IMPs in general contribute to innovation success but in particular the IMPS 'external technology intelligence gathering' and 'technology and product portfolio management' are relevant. In addition, they conclude that: "the use and effectiveness of most IMPs varies by industry" (p. 1) and therefore advise innovation managers that with regard to selecting and implementing IMPs into their organization they "must be highly selective" (idem). IMPs are here to be considered success factors although we consider the term 'practices' more modest and less absolute. Apparently, that also gives way to a much lesser strict use of these practices by emphasizing, as the authors do, to vary the practices per industry.

Given the importance of innovation for companies it is not surprising that so many studies tried to find the philosopher's stone of management in general and of innovation in particular. Knowing those principles that explain and predict business success can be put at the same line as trying to reach unachievable goals such as knowing the meaning of life or being able to predict the future correctly. Indeed, the validity of these success factors seem to be limited and it might be therefore more interesting and relevant to study the underlying mechanisms that explain this sequence of various factors that explain why some companies are highly innovative (for a period) and others not.

We have used several terms such as business principles, success factors, best (good) practices, and determinants of success and failure of innovation. We do not wish to start a semantic discussion, so we group these different terms under the umbrella of *success factors* since they all describe in a concise way how and why companies have achieved (innovation) success. However, a difference should be made between studies explicitly aimed at finding success factors and studies in which practices of innovation management are described by, for instance, developing a typology (e.g., Medina et al., 2005). The outcomes of these latter studies could be seen as a first step towards contextual innovation management.

Another point is the different roles the success factors can have. For scientists, success factors are meant to explain or describe innovation processes at organizations. For consultants the success factors provide vital knowledge to advise their clients. These different roles can be put on a continuum starting with describing successful innovation processes, then explaining them, and then prescribing them. So, these success factors range between a *positive* and a *normative* view on innovation management.

Both describing and prescribing success factors for innovation means that innovation should be measured by means of 'monitoring' or 'evaluating'. Monitoring is the most descriptive way of looking at innovation processes since, in principle, it has a neutral stance towards the innovation processes it describes. Evaluating is much more judgmental about the processes since it attempts to characterize the innovation processes in terms of bad or good (or something in between). Once again, the difference between both approaches can be very small. Describing innovation processes in a neutral way without drawing conclusions might be correct from a scientific perspective but has less value for changing and improving innovation. Evaluating innovation processes provides many more clues about the state of innovation and how this possibly can be altered. However, to measure and improve the right aspects one needs to have the right indicators for which we first have to describe the essential parts of the innovation process. This connection does not necessarily have to be made as can be seen in a study by Adams et al. (2006), who have studied indicators to measure innovation and found that these are in principle only meant for describing how innovation management takes place and not how they should (or should not) take place.

Box 2.2   Success Factors Taken Out of Context

The aforementioned Henry Chesbrough (see also Box 1.1.) wrote a book entitled *Open Innovation* in 2003 in which he describes a new innovation paradigm. The book received a lot of positive attention, both from the scientific and the commercial angle. Chesbrough's description of how certain companies 'open up' their innovation processes has since become so widely adopted that the open innovation paradigm not only has a descriptive but also a prescriptive character. In other words, the open innovation paradigm has become an essential part of a list of success factors that are supposed to optimize the quality of innovation processes in companies. However, the question is whether Chesbrough intended that. Does every company really have to switch to open innovation? Is every industry suited for open innovation? Already in the introduction to his book, Chesbrough writes that it is not the case that all companies apply the principles of open innovation (p. xxvii). In fact, Chesbrough places different industries on a continuum where open innovation is applied on the one hand and closed innovation on the other. In this way he comes to an overview of contextual conditions that indicate whether open or closed innovation should be applied (p. xxviii):

Closed innovation	Open Innovation
Largely internal ideas for innovation	Mainly external ideas
Limited labor mobility	High labor mobility
Little venture capital	A lot of venture capital
Few and weak start-ups	Numerous start-ups
Universities are not important	Universities are important

Another issue is that most measurements or evaluations of innovation are about the characteristics of the innovative product or service and less about the innovation process or the "*permanent and global* innovation management of the company" (Rejeb et al., 2008, p. 839). Measuring the innovation process itself (i.e., the throughput, instead of the input to it and the output from it) is much more difficult because one has to be able to link "the resources to the outcomes of the innovation process" (idem.). In our view this is impossible if one strives to do it in a quantitative way, which is often the case given the large emphasis of the economic view on studying innovation. Just relating the input of an innovation process to its output by regression or correlation will not result in useful clues for innovation managers to optimize their innovation processes (see also Chapter 6, section 6.4). Especially input indicators such as amount of patents held by an organization or R&D expenditures do not say much about the innovative capacities of an organization (Kleinknecht et al., 2002). Also, the shift in defining innovation from just a technical invention towards defining innovation as a new product, service, organization, business model or design as well, all of which the technical qualities are not necessarily the most essential ones (see: Van der Duin et al., 2005), also impact the measurement of innovation. Indeed, the increasing attention of innovation studies and of organizations to *innovation systems* even more broadens the range of (success) factors that we should measure to understand or improve, and shifts the unit of analysis from organization to system (of which the organization becomes a part of). For example, instead of looking at patents or having the most intelligent researchers, being able to make quick and good relations with organizations from other industries might become a much more relevant innovation indicator or success factor. This broadening of the list of indicators also could make measuring too complex or even less relevant and instead we might start focusing on better *understanding* the innovation process itself (Medina et al., 2005, p. 272).

Lastly, the search for success factors is indeed often about success and not about failure factors. After all, one could also look for failure factors and by reversing them find the success factors, but for some reason that does not happen. Looking for success factors might indeed be the easiest and most efficient way of getting hold of business success. People are not inclined to talk about failures or their mistakes. And the archive for 'failed innovation processes' is often non-existent; we are not eager to keep records of it and don't like to be reminded of those things that failed and that we were forced to abandon. Getting rid of everything that refers to that might be a psychological trick to forget the failures and focus on the success. Failed innovation processes do not exist anymore whereas the successful innovation processes can be found back in the high turnover and profit figures of an organization. A fine example of this positive line of thinking is a study by Burgers et al. (2008) titled: 'Why new business development project fail: coping with the differences of technological versus market knowledge', for which they researched eight new business development projects, all of which "provided significant revenues" (p. 61), which does not indicate that they were failed business development projects. . . .

A somewhat different explanation would be that looking for things within an organization that went well yields more and better data than asking about what went wrong. The American management scientist David Cooperrider discovered this effect when he did research in a hospital in the United States. Instead of looking for what went wrong and looking for how to solve problems, the research approach he took focused on what went right. Starting with this research, a research approach was developed called 'Appreciative inquiry' (see Cooperrider et al., 1999), which indeed aimed at finding out what works and how people think about certain issues, thereby taking a positive perspective. The search for success factors for innovation processes often follows this 'philosophy'.

2.3 Reviewing Success Factors

Business life is not as easy as the studies on success factors suggest. Having one set of success factors that is valid for a long period suggests that *both* organizations and contexts are constant for a long period. Given the tremendous changes in society, industry, and organizations, we cannot hold this view.

Organizations have different strengths and weaknesses and face different problems and dilemmas, and therefore benefit from a different way of doing business: "innovation challenges differ from firm to firm, and otherwise commonly followed advice can be wasteful, even harmful, if applied to the wrong situations" (Hansen and Birkinshaw, 2007, p. 2). Indeed, innovation practices are found to vary with firm size, sector, and country (Evangelista and Mastrostefano, 2006). Pohlmann (2005) explains this diversity of innovation models being used mainly by differences in cultural backgrounds of countries.

Thinking in success factors generally assumes that organizations resemble each other, which is called 'organizational nomorphism' (Di Maggio and Powell, 1983). Benchmarking, a management tool that contributes to the notion that organizations are similar, is a widely used practice in business and management. Organizations often look at each other, perhaps with the goal to look for differences, but mostly the aim is to learn from each other, and by applying those lessons results in organizations that more and more resemble each other. That is, learning then means copying each other's 'best' practices which contributes to their resemblance. This tendency of resembling is then the result of deliberate decisions and actions taken by managers who are eagerly, and perhaps sometimes desperately, looking for better ways to organize and carry out their business and think that that knowledge ways can be found within other organizations. The pervasiveness of benchmarking in management means that the one-size-fits-all-approach is reinforcing itself, resulting in organizational neomorphism. Benchmarking assumes that organizations are predominantly comparable, which raises the question if and which organizational or environmental elements are comparable. Some organizations might be comparable since they compete in the same market and hence benchmarking might be useful then.

But, copying the management approach of other organizations is not a very effective way to become successful if organizations operate in different business and societal environments. Moreover, the outcomes of benchmarking studies are based on historical situations. For instance, case studies of successful companies give a clear insight in why and how an organization has become successful, but these case studies are historical descriptions and therefore are not automatically applicable to present or future times when the environment and an organization has changed. Learning the business lessons from the past does not offer good guidelines to manage businesses in the future.

Box 2.3   Success Factors and Our Capitalist System

It is remarkable to note that this *seeking* for success factors to become successful is in sharp contrast with another popular *search* activity done by many organizations, that is to find out how it can distinguish itself from other organizations. One could argue that these quests are different from each other since the first one (i.e., for eternal success factors) has a process character (i.e., *how* to organize and innovate successfully), while the second one is about content (i.e., *what* makes a company successful). Especially management scientists involved with research on strategy often emphasize the need for companies to develop a strategy that significantly differs from competitors to limit competitive pressures and creative a safe 'niche' in which companies can operate more or less in a protected manner. In that niche they can build up solid and constant relationships with their customers, who will not easily and quickly switch to other suppliers, and in which they have sufficient time to develop their own new products and services which, in turn, safeguards this niche. Ironically, it appears as if the most important strategy for companies, the dominant symbols and carriers of our capitalist system, is to adopt strategies to decrease the level of competition, while competition is one of the main characteristics of that same capitalist system.

In addition to the historical fallacy of 'success cases', the limited value of it can also be illustrated by the limitation of the case-study *method* itself. The case-study method is a very often applied research method in management studies, aimed at discovering the deeper mechanisms and principles of empirical practices and phenomena. It is very functional in *explorative* research of which the aim is not to confirm, test, or validate the existing body of knowledge, but to look for new factors, explanations, or mechanisms that describe or explain our (social) world. It mainly tries to find the particular aspects of a case rather than the general aspects that are typical for many cases in general. External validity in this type of research seems less important than internal and construct validity.

With doing a case-study one tries to gain in-depth knowledge about how an organization functions. Since other organizations are left out, the case conclusions can be considered valid for that specific case. The *statistical* generalization, as it is called, for case studies is indeed rather low. *Theoretical* generalization, as it is called, is determining to what extent the case conclusions also hold for other, non-researched organizations by assessing to what extent the characteristics of the case and the non-research cases are comparable. Given the important place and influence we attach to the environment of an organization we would argue that this environment is essential for deciding whether the outcomes of the case study are also externally valid. Not surprisingly, specific organizational characteristics will have a less prominent place in deciding which factors are relevant for determining external validity. By concluding that the found success factors in a case study are *true* success factors, meaning that they go beyond the researched case (i.e., the organization), is applying statistical generalization. We hold the opinion that applying this type of generalization wrongly extends the found success factors to non-researched cases. Only theoretical generalizations can yield sensible conclusions about if and to what extent found success factor *might* also be applicable to non-researched cases, thereby extending the validity of the success factor. However, since, non-researched cases are often part of a different environment (context), theoretical generalizations are not possible. Doing case studies, to conclude, is not a good way to find generalizable success factors. But (as we will see in Chapter 3) it is indeed a good way to describe and explain why a certain company uses a specific approach to innovation management.

2.4 Concluding Remarks

That success factors work for a certain period and for a certain organization does not mean that they will work again or for other organizations. Success factors for certain organizations cannot simply be compared with those of other organizations. Also, success factors are difficult to predict. Factors that at one point in time are considered strange might later turn out to be important. Brilliant ideas may initially be considered strange but that does not mean that all current strange ideas will ultimately turn out to be brilliant.

Nevertheless, many possible success factors can or will be considered as strange since they are initially applied by a single organization before becoming common practice. Dell was the first (computer) company to innovate its supply chain radically; Toyota was the first (automotive) company to apply Kaizen to its innovation process; and Semler was the first company to let its employees decide themselves on their working times and height of salary. At first, these organizations were looked at as exotic and perhaps obscure since they deviated significantly from mainstream management practices. But their business success turned their strange and deviant considered business principles into factors that inspired many companies.

We do not think that business success is based on a fixed set of rules or principles but that business success needs to be discovered, explained, and implemented constantly. Within the back of our mind that 'change is the only constant', we strive to find out how these business principles develop over time and, moreover, how these different business principles relate to different kinds of contexts. However, given that business success consists of many different aspects, we limit ourselves in this book to the field of innovation management. In this field "there is no grail, no algorithm, and no one model for increasing the capacity for breakthrough innovation in research-intensive companies" (Weick and Jain, 2014, p. 5).

We hold the opinion that innovation management *should* be contextual, meaning that the way companies should innovate in a successful way is in line with the demands and/or requirements put upon them by the context or environment in which companies operate. Since this context is not constant, companies should not only adapt to this context but also change their innovation principles according to this changing context. This means that these principles are not fixed but change over *time* and differ per *context*. Success factors are temporal and local phenomena, limiting their broader applicability and thereby questioning their very nature as success factor, which suggests a much more universal applicability, both in time and in place.

Note

1 For example, McGourty et al. (1996) devote an entire article just to investigating and defining the positive role of the culture of an organization in managing innovation.

3 From Contingency to Contextual

The faith in success factors is persistent and widespread. In contrast, contingency-theory is a field in management science that adopts the premise that companies should adapt their organization and strategy to the environment or the context. Contingency theory refutes the idea of a generic and fixed set of success factors. The fact that the environment changes means that companies have to change too. In the natural sciences, changes can be explained using a fixed and generally valid set of equations. In the social sciences, to which management science belongs, change means that different variables and different relationships between them become important, and hence the set of equations to explain the phenomena of change are themselves changing. The contingency perspective is a very relevant perspective to explore and develop specific innovation management approaches that fit particular companies and their environment.

3.1 Introduction: Contingency Theory

The notion that business success in general and innovation success in particular can be explained by a general and fixed set of success factors is widely held. In this book, we argue that it is better to consider the way that organizations innovate as context dependent. This notion is theoretically and scientifically rooted in a management theory known as 'contingency theory'.

As is the case with many scientific theories, it is not always clear who developed the first ideas and hence can be called the grandfather or grandmother. A classical reference is the work of Paul R. Lawrence and Jay W. Lorsch who with their 1967 book 'Organization and environment' hoped to "renew interest in contingency theory" (Lawrence and Lorsch, 1967, p. xii). They refer to scientists such as T. Burns and G.M. Stalker (see section 3.5) and others (including the famous management scientist Alfred Chandler) who have laid down the foundation of contingency theory. They give credit to Fred Fiedler for using the term 'contingency', and they claim (we think rightfully) in the preface that their book changed the basic issue to "what management style and organization form is best suited to a particular situation?" More specifically, the focus was on the fit between an organization and its environment (p. ix).

Pennings (1992, p. 268) states that "contingency holds that for organizations to be effective there has to be a goodness of fit between its structural design and the conditions of the environment" (see also Drazin and Van de Ven, 1985, p. 515). Donaldson, in his seminal book on contingency, states that "(T)he essence of the contingency paradigm is that organizational effectiveness results from fitting characteristics of the organization, such as its structure, to contingencies that reflect the situation of the organization"(2001, p. 1). Elsewhere, Donaldson (1999) is even more clear: "Contingency theory states that there is no single organizational structure that is highly effective for all organizations" (p. 51).[1] Donaldson indicates that contingency factors need to fit major organizational choices in order to be effective. These contingency factors are considered to constitute elements of the environment with which organizations must align their choices. Moreover, given the possible variation in factors, not only for each environment but also over time, these variations of factors prevent a 'one-size-fits-all-approach'. In addition, Zeithaml et al. (1993) state that "the essential premise of the contingency approach is that effectiveness, broadly defined as organizational adaptation and survival . . ., can be achieved in more than one way" (p. 39). This does not give rise to an 'anything goes' way of management. Variations in effectiveness can be very wide but they are not random: "Effectiveness depends on the appropriate matching of contingency factors with internal organizational designs that can allow appropriate responses to the environment" (idem., p. 40).

Zooming in on the term *contingent*, Jaffee (2001, p. 210) states that "(W)hen something is said to be 'contingent' it means that it *depends* upon events or circumstances". Jaffee then applies it specific to organizations: "*contingency* means that the effectiveness of a particular organizational structure or strategy depends upon the presence or absence of other factors" (idem.). Fry and Smith (1987) point to the close relationship between the terms *contingency* and *congruence* in developing theory. They state that for an organization to reach its goals, congruence is required between various organizational components, such as between structure and technology or between strategy and environment (p. 117). Indeed, this looks a lot like contingency, but according to Fry and Smith "congruence is defined by the laws of relationship of a theory's variables, and . . . contingency is defined by the system states where the integrity of the system is maintained" (p. 117). In our words: contingency focuses on the relation between an organization and its environment, while congruence looks more at the intra-organizational relations. Contingency has a more holistic nature than congruence, in that sense.

These definitions clearly describe contingency theory, although in a rather general way. A more abstract definition describes contingency theory as a relationship between two sets of variables, which predicts effectiveness, assuming an interaction between the two sets of predictor variables (Pennings, 1987, p. 225).

As we see in the various definitions, various concepts are present, such as fit, design, and environment. For example, Fry and Smith (1987, p. 117) report on many different contingency-type studies all addressing how organizations *fit* the environment using many different terms for this 'fit' such as matching, dictation, aligning, clustering, consistency, and (again) congruency. Apparently, the *relationship* between the organization and environment is at the heart of contingency-theory. Indeed, according to Gebhardt (2005, p. 21) innovativeness is perceived as the best structural fit to an ever-changing environment", meaning that not only innovation itself should be viewed from a contingency perspective but that innovating organizations constantly adjust themselves to a changing environment. In addition, Drazin and Van de Ven (1985) state that 'fit' is the key proposition of the 'contingent proposition'.

If we look at contingency from a purely organization theoretical perspective then it is considered by Astley and Van de Ven (1983) to be part of the system-structural view to which also systems theory and structural functionalism belong. More particularly, this view is characterized by Astley and Van de Ven as "divide and integrate roles to adapt subsystems to changes in environment, technology size, and resource needs", the organizational behavior is "determined, constrained, and adaptive", and the role of the manager is 'reactive' (idem, p. 247; see also: Hrebiniak and Joyce (1985)).

Of course, contingency theory is not without criticism. Schoonhoven (1981, pp. 350–353) lists five problems. In his view, contingency is not a theory but more an "orienting strategy or metatheory" and the "theoretical statements" made by contingency theory "fail to provide any clues about the specific form of the interaction intended". The thorough criticism of Schoonhoven would justify an equal thorough discussion and response, but as we will clarify in section 3.6 we do not accept the 'full' contingency theory but predominantly consider its scientific background which inspires us and other innovation management scholars to consider innovation management contextually. Furthermore, the criticism by Schoonhoven is aimed at the mathematical and causal aspects of contingency theory, two aspects that we give much less emphasis in our description of contextual innovation management. That is, we will pay specific attention to the *mechanisms, workings,* and *processes* of contextual innovation, which require a more qualitative approach.

3.2 Contingency Theory and Research Strategies

Academic freedom allows each management scientist to choose his or her own research strategy. Choices for research strategies are often made based on the personal skills and experiences of the researcher, on the personal view of a scientist on the world in general, and on the unit of analysis in particular. However, given the character of contingency theory itself, we have the opinion that a case-based research approach is the best way to start exploring contingencies. Our opinion is confirmed by Donaldson (1999, p. 51): "the task of contingency research is to *identify* (our italics) the particular contingency factor or factors to which each particular aspect of organizational structure needs to fit". Identification refers to exploring relationships rather than testing hypothesized relationships. An important reason for our opinion is that case-study research predominantly aims at finding particular relationships that hold in the unique situation of one organization, rather than the aim to test generally valid relationships holding for many organizations in different situations.

If we exaggerate a little bit by considering explorative (qualitative, inductive) and explanatory (quantitative, deductive) as opposites, indeed as black and white, we can hold that case-study research is more focused on gaining in-depth knowledge, and is therefore suitable for *identifying* contingencies in management science. After the identification of a contingency in one case, further case studies can explore contingencies in other cases. But given the richness of data about one specific case, contingencies are often highly case-specific. Case studies need to have more 'diverse' or 'thick' data since the uniqueness of organizations (i.e., their structure, strategy, innovation management) requires that many factors (e.g., history, management team, strategy) should be taken into account (Harrigan, 1983, p. 398). A single case-study research design can thus find a completely unique contingency. Such a result cannot simply be generalized to other cases. However, generalizability is possible when a larger set of heterogeneous cases, representing the variety of cases in a population, explores many of such contingencies. If the number of cases is large enough, saturation appears when no new contingencies are found in subsequent cases. A heterogeneous set of cases in a multiple case study research design can hence yield a generalizable result: a complete set of contingencies. Generalizability then means that contingencies in specific cases are a subset of the complete and larger set of contingencies. Inevitably, such contingencies are formulated on a bit more abstract or general level. The more abstract and generic contingencies that appear from a multiple-case study research design can then serve as hypotheses to be tested in a larger set of cases as part of a more deductive, testing, and quantitative type of research design. In such a design the strength or chance of appearance of a contingency can be assessed and found to be generalizable to a larger population of cases.[2] This is a different type of generalizability than we find in quantitative research!

So, both types of research—explorative (qualitative, inductive) and explanatory research (quantitative, deductive)—have a role in finding contingencies. The explorative research can do different things. It can help to identify new contingencies and to understand why a certain factor can be considered a contingency factor, and how and by which mechanisms it affects organization (or innovation) performance. The richness of data in a case study does allow (innovation) managers to use these contingency factors as organizational 'tools'. Finally, the explorative research, in the form of a multiple case-study design, can help formulate a set of contingencies, a subset of which can be found in singular cases. The explanatory work can test various hypotheses regarding relationships between possible contingency factors and organizational performance in a larger subset of cases (e.g., Damanpour, 1996).

3.3 Contextual Innovation Management, Management Theory, and Management Practice

It is not always clear what the origins of a specific management theory are since these theories are not only generated by empirical research in organizations but are also inspired by organizational practices. The combination of these origins creates a kind of dialectical process by which the management theory is being improved in a cycle of testing and validation. Both organizations and scientists profit from this interaction. Managers in organizations profit because they can apply a validated body of knowledge and do not have to develop their own framework guiding managerial activities. Scientists benefit because applying the theories in practice provides feedback that can be used to validate their theories. It is important that this feedback process does not result in a kind of 'official theory' in the organization (see also Salaman and Storey, 2002). Being critical to one's own routines and practices is vital for taking a contextual approach since that requires a constant update of how management processes should be carried out. At the same time, it is possible that there is no specific theory available so that managers have to develop their own ideas, practices, and frameworks which are then 'discovered' by scientists who formalize those into abstract theories. One could describe both types of processes as inductive *and* deductive but one must note that these processes intertwine and therefore influence each other. An important condition for this dialectical process to take place is of course that both management scientists and managers are open to each other's ideas, knowledge, and experiences to facilitate a balanced exchange.

A consequence of this dialectical process is that management theories cannot easily be categorized as either prescriptive or descriptive. The nature of a management theory might depend on whether the theory is guiding managerial practices (prescriptive or normative) or the theory is focused on how organizations are managed in practice (descriptive or positive). A clear example of the 'confused background' of a management theory in the field of innovation is the 'open innovation' theory by Henry Chesbrough (2003) who initially based his theory about the extensive exchange of innovation-related knowledge between organizations (companies) on case studies at Intel and IBM. Nowadays, his theory currently has so many 'followers' that it has changed or extended from a descriptive one into a prescriptive one (see also. Ghoshal, 2005, p. 77),[3]

With regard to the theory of contextual innovation management: it is in between descriptive and prescriptive, having elements of both approaches. That is, the absence of fixed success formulas can point to a descriptive approach since it is based on the empirical observations that these formulas do not exist (or only for a short while and in a specific industry). The prescriptive element of it is not the contextual factors themselves; it is rather the *notion* of taking a contextual approach to managing organizations and innovation processes. Indeed, there are empirical studies that conclude that organizations that have a diverse set of innovation management approaches perform better than companies who do not (e.g., Barczak et al., 2009).

We just described this dialectical relationship between theory and practice of management theories in a quite unproblematic fashion. However, Benson (1977) states that this "interplay between practical interests and scholarship" (p. 16) could result in a 'coherent system', but at the same time this might lead to a situation in which the specific nature of an organizational theory (human relations, structural-functional, and open systems) only describes a specific aspect of an organizational structure and process. We think that this myopic process is also fueled by another tendency in the scientific community: the tendency to specialize, since that is considered by many scholars the best way to increase the scientific validity of their work and improve their personal citation-score and publication ranking. This 'danger' of a coherent but closed system that, contrary to its suggestion, has a limited applicability to understanding organizations as a whole, may also apply to the theory of contextual innovation management. The set of contextual factors will always be limited due to the wish to make it applicable in practice, thereby unknowingly adding to the aforementioned specialization trend in management science. In addition, contextual innovation management is devoted to managing innovation processes that are just a part of the total set of managerial activities of an organization. Nevertheless, the theory of contextual innovation management is indeed touching a more encompassing framework than Benson (1977) is looking for. Contextual innovation management is not prescribing which factors (or variables) are valid. The theory of contextual innovation management predominantly advises both scientists and companies to enter a process to look for those contextual factors that are relevant to them. In addition, the relevant contextual factors are not constant but change depending on how (and how fast) the environment (context) of the organization is changing. This makes the theory of contextual innovation management more flexible than most other organizational theories.

If organizations apply contextual innovation management then the variety in innovation management perspective will increase. Companies will distinguish themselves and search for their market niche (see also: section 2.3). In such a situation, benchmarking of organizations will become less valuable and important. Comparing (or benchmarking) organizations will then not so much be any more about comparing organizational success factors, but about how 'different' companies organize their innovation management in a comparable context. The context becomes then the most important criterion to categorize organizations instead of, for instance, the type of business they are in or what type of customers they service.

3.4 Applications of Contingency Theory in Management Science

The rather abstract and general character of contingency theory has enabled many applications in different subfields of management ranging from classical organization theory to more specific corners of management such as the development of software products. A simple search in databases of scientific journals using search terms such as contingency, contextual, and management in titles of articles on management and organization studies in the period from 2000 to 2016 results in dozens of articles. In the following we just give a few examples to illustrate the broadness of applications of contingency theory in the field of management.

- Shenhar (2001) explores 'classical contingency' domains in the field of project management. His contingency framework for different ways of project management distinguishes between four levels of technological uncertainty (low, medium, high, super high) and three levels of system complexity (an assembly project, a system project, an array project).
- O'Reilly and Tushman (2013, p. 9) distinguish different types of ambidexterity: sequential, simultaneous (or structural), and contextual.[4] Without explicitly referring to contingency theory, the extent to which a particular style of ambidexterity is useful to an organization depends on the type of environment: stable, dynamic, fast, slower.
- Keller (1994) describes a study among 98 R&D project groups and finds support "for the contingency theory hypothesis that the fit between a task technology's non-routiness and information-processing needs will predict project performance" (p. 167).
- Lichtenthaler (2005) investigated which contingency factors are relevant and significant in the effectiveness of technology intelligence methods that are being used by 25 leading European and North American companies. The strategic importance of a (future) issue,

the fit of a method with the chosen time horizon, the intention of individual or organizational learning, the corporate decision making style, and the corporate culture seem to be valid contingency factors.

- Gassmann and Von Zedtwitz (1999b) have researched the possible ways of organizing virtual teams in R&D settings using a contingency approach. The have identified four forms of virtual team organization that are based on four contingent determinants: type of innovation, systemic nature of the project, the mode of knowledge involved, and the degree of resource bundling.

- Farneti and Young (2008) research how municipalities manage the outsourcing of risks using a contingency approach. They conclude that municipalities need different types of governance models depending on the nature (i.e., citizen sensitivity to risk) and amount of risk.

- Zott and Amit (2008) research what the contingent effects are of "product market strategy and business model choices on firm performance" (p. 1). They conclude that both are 'distinct constructs that affect the firms' market value', that both concepts are complimentary instead of each other's substitutes, and that the role of the firm's business model is contingent in the determination of its market value (p. 19).

3.5 Applications of Contingency Theory in Innovation Management

In addition to the application of contingency theory to management topics such as knowledge management and project management, it has also been applied to innovation management specifically. In the following we present a few illustrative examples. Applying contingency *thinking* to innovation is not a new phenomenon, by the way. Already in 1961, Burns and Stalker (see also section 3.1) wrote in the preface to the second edition of their book *The Management of Innovation*:

> If the form of management is properly to be seen as dependent on the situation the concern is trying to meet, it follows that there is no single set of principles for 'good organization', an ideal type of management system which can serve as a model to which administrative practice should, or could in time, approximate.
>
> (p. vii-viii)

This history of applications of contingency theory to innovation has resulted in several studies of which we give here four examples:

- Chapman et al. (2001) investigate which elements influence continuous improvement in product innovation. They find that relevant variables such as behavior, levers, and performance are influenced by knowledge management (contingency variable) in which a 'locally based'-approach to knowledge management requires, for example, an emphasis on high-technology and inter-firm connections, while for a 'global system' approach it is advisable to implement organizational integrative levers and computer based technologies (p. 23).

- Souitaris (2000) carried out a contingency-type of research of which the "aim is to test the applicability of Pavitt's taxonomy for a contingency theory on the determinants of innovation" (p. 339). He concludes that different groups of industrial sectors do not only relate to the type of technological pattern they are part of, but that every type of sector relates to other, different (contingency) variables such as understanding the market ('supplier dominated' sector), ability to finance projects ('scale-intensive firms'), and licensing ('science-based firms') (p. 344).

- Khurum et al. (2015) report on a study into the development processes of three software products developed by different companies. Next to stating that "innovation processes cannot be standardized, but are contextual in nature" (p. 595), their main findings are that the following contextual factors are important with regard to innovation processes in the software industry: inherent properties of software, survival threat, the presence or absence of software and business legacy, and entrepreneurial power and capabilities.

- Tidd and Thuriaux-Alemán (2016) conclude that the patterns of practices (usage) of innovation management vary across sectors and that there is a "positive relationship between the use of innovation management practices and innovation outcomes" (p. 1). Just a few practices seem to be universally positive: external technology intelligence gathering, and technology and product portfolio management (idem.). Given the potential of a more widespread use of (specific) innovation management practices, they recommend innovation managers "to be selective in their choice of technique based on the innovation opportunities and technology challenges" (p. 14).

3.6 From Contingency to Contextual Innovation Management[5]

As we said at the beginning of this chapter, we consider contingency theory as the theoretical and science-philosophical foundation of contextual innovation management. Strictly speaking, it is difficult to speak of 'the' contingency theory. Various contingency factors are distinguished for different management-related subjects. The 'classic' contingency factors came from studies into organizational structure and focused on size and complexity. Applying the contingency approach to innovation management will probably yield different contingency factors. Indeed, we do

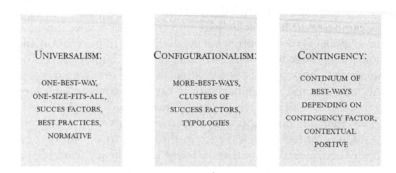

Figure 3.1 Various Approaches to Management

not, as we see often with applications of contingency theory, assume the existence of a single contingency factor but rather consider a set of related contingency factors explaining the (required) differences in approaches to innovation management.

Figure 3.1 presents three approaches to management on a continuum, from a unique set of success factors (universalism), via a combined cluster of success factors (configurationalism), to a series of contingency factors that have a unique combination (match) with the organizational factor.[6] Universalism explains the success of a company by following one or more success factors (see Chapter 2). Configurationalism argues that success factors can be combined into meaningful clusters ('configurations'). In principle, companies that find themselves in one of those clusters are successful, while other companies have a wrong cocktail of (inconsistent) success factors. Well-known examples of clusters are the organization typology proposed by Henry Mintzberg and the various strategies of Michael Porter.[7]

Universalism assumes that there is a (unique) optimum that applies to every company, while configurationalism argues that there are various, local, and discrete optimums, which means that the choice of optimum is less important as long as the choice is made with conviction and the company does not attempt to formulate a compromise between the various local optimums. Finally, there is the contingency approach that is matched to the contingency factor on the basis of the status of the independent variable (in this case a characteristic of the organization, such as the way it innovates or the level of technological uncertainty). Although contextual innovation management is founded on contingency theory we locate contextual innovation management predominantly in the sphere of configurationalism because we think that there is no single unique contingency factor explaining or prescribing the best way of innovation management and that a more plural approach rightfully acknowledges the complexity of how to manage innovation. Consider the view of Zeithaml et al. (1993), who consider contingency-theories as a "mid-range theories between the two extreme views which state either that universal principles of organisation and management exist or that each organisation is unique and each situation must be analysed separately" (p. 37). So, according to these authors there is in Figure 3.1. a category to the right of contingency and the configurationalism and contingency are closer to each other than we here suggest. Goffee and Jones (2011) especially point out the practical need of finding a middle way with regard to (strategic) leadership, since given "that there are endless contingencies in life, there are endless varieties of leadership. . . . the beleaguered executive looking for a model to help him is hopelessly lost" (p. 85).

Contextual innovation management rests on the notion that the business world is not a closed system, such as a laboratory system in which performing identical experiments result in identical outcomes, but an open system (see: Bhaskar, 1975) in which limiting the operating area of the unit of analysis under study is prevented as much as possible. Of course, certain limitations need to be made to make sure that (scientific) research is practically possible but considering the unit of analysis *within* an open system enables the detection of many relevant factors. In that sense, applying a contingency approach to innovation management requires an explorative approach of doing research since finding and applying the right set of contingency factors is the core of contingency thinking. After finding the relevant contextual factors, explanatory research needs to be carried out to find out which contextual factors are the most relevant and how strong the relationships are between these factors, how they impact the organization, and how they relate to the fit between the environment (the context) and the way an organization manages innovation processes. As such, research into contingency is in line with a cyclic approach to research in which induction (exploratory research) and deduction are carried out iteratively.

3.7 Contextual Innovation Management and Social Constructivism

In contextual innovation management, the different perspectives of employees involved with innovation management play an important role. Often within a single organization, different perceptions on the context of the organization are present, resulting in various views on how the organization should fit innovation processes to the context. Therefore, we think that contextual innovation management is in line with a social constructivist view on knowledge production. In this view, it is argued that reality is not independent from our views, perspectives, and opinions, but that its form and nature is *constructed* (or produced) by how people think about this (their) reality, by how they speak about this (their) reality, and how they decide upon this perceived and labeled reality. Consequently, the social constructivist view on reality will result in multiple realities since individuals or groups of individuals will not always 'agree' on what reality is, let alone on what it should be. Whether this diversity in constructions is considered a problem depends on to what extent someone agrees with this particular view on reality. If that someone thinks he or she has a rather 'objective' view on reality then this standpoint will be difficult to accept since the social constructivist view denies a singular, objective view on reality. In addition, the acceptance of this philosophy also depends on the issue of whether or not people hold different opinions or different perspectives on reality. One could argue, for instance, that in a decision-making process within an organization in the exploring phases of solving a problem or researching an opportunity, the constructivist view is advisable since it is good to look at the issue at stake from different angles and to make sure that as many as possible of the related factors are being mapped. But the more a decision-making process is approaching its final decision-making point and its subsequent implementation, the less fruitful it might be to hold diverse views and opinions since a good decision often is regarded as a decision that leaves no room for interpretation.

In particular, according to Mir and Watson (2000, pp. 942–944) the 'constructivist methodology' is characterized by six characteristics: 1) theory-driven knowledge; 2) no separation between subject and object; 3) no separation between theory and practice; 4) researchers are and cannot be 'objective' or value-neutral; 5) "(R)esearch occurs within a 'community'", and 6) a distinction between a methodology and a method, which means that "a researcher who is anchored in constructivist methodology may employ a variety of methods including statistical analysis" (p. 944). As said, we consider contextual innovation management in essence as social constructivism but we admit that not each of the six characteristics of Mir and Watson is line with this. For instance, we do think that the constructivist methodology relates to certain research methods or approaches with regard to contextual innovation (see section 3.2) and we also think that research based on contextual innovation not necessarily have to start with theory. Nevertheless, contextual innovation does address sufficiently the other four aspects to be regarded as social constructivist. That is, it does not separate (strongly) between object and subject (see section 3.2); researchers are indeed not value neutral since the specific factors of contextual innovation can be the result of certain practices and 'organizational power relations' (see section 5.2) that make the separation between theory and practice difficult to achieve.

One could also argue that having different views on reality is a 'fact' of life. Reality is dynamic because it changes almost constantly, which makes every view or interpretation of it time- and context-bounded. To give an example from economics, unemployment is a constant factor of our (capitalist) economy and society. However, its causes have changed over time. In the 1920s and 1930s, it was the result of low demand whereas in the 1970s and 1980s it was the result of a qualitative mismatch between demand and supply of labor. Moreover, it is expected that in the future (rising) unemployment will be the result of laborsaving technologies such as robotization and artificial intelligence. In addition, reality is multidimensional since people hold different social positions and are therefore confronted by different aspects of reality. Especially within organizations (contexts), different employees have different tools and different responsibilities, and carry out different tasks. These differences will not only be relevant to how innovation management should be carried out but also to the strategic issue of how important innovation is for the organization and to what extent the organization should be innovative.

From a purely scientific perspective, one could argue that the social constructivist view will not have many proponents among natural scientists since their predominant view on nature (their principal unit of analysis) is that of an objective phenomenon which does not give much room to different interpretations and (therefore) is also considered quantitatively. In the social sciences, of which we consider innovation often to be considered a part (see Fagerberg and Verspagen, 2009), it is a different situation since social phenomena lend themselves more easily to different viewpoints, which also allows for a more qualitative approach to studying these social phenomena.

3.8 Concluding Remarks

The scientific-historical background of contextual approach to innovation management goes back quite far. It is rooted in contingency theory, which dealt with organizational change regarding (technological) changes in the environment of the organization, but did not immediately focus on innovation management. Nevertheless, one of the first books on innovation already adopted a contingency approach. Contingency theory and a contextual approach to innovation management as well, are particularly suited for research strategies that try to find the particular instead of the general. Case research, therefore, is a good and often-used research strategy for finding the relevant contextual factors as long as one does not extend the findings to other, non-researched cases (as is often done in the 'best-practices' literature discussed in Chapter 2). In addition, a theory of contextual innovation management is rooted and fueled both by management science and by the practices of innovation managers at organizations, which gives it both a descriptive (explaining) and prescriptive character. In this book we do not comply fully with the contingency approach but base the theory of contextual innovation management on a moderate version of it, namely configurationalism. This management approach is positioned in between contingency and universalism (which is thinking in terms of 'one best way'). It must be said, of course, that contextual innovation management leans far more towards contingency than to universalism. Lastly, contextual innovation management is based on a social constructivist view on reality, which means that the practice of innovation is very much driven by how innovation managers perceive the reality of their business and subsequently decide about how to innovate.

Notes

1 In our view, and as we will see in Chapter 4, organization is a contextual factor for innovation processes.
2 Actually, a contingency factor gaining a high validity might ultimately even turn into a success factor. . . .
3 Trott and Hartmann (2009; see also Box 1.1) criticize the newness of the open-innovation concept claiming that it dates back a long time, by which they show this confused historical background and that these dialectical processes between management practice and management theory can take quite some time. In addition, Torkkeli et al. (2009) state that 'open innovation' needs to be approached from a contingency perspective, in particular with regard to the buying and selling of knowledge making 'openness' and 'closeness' more relative terms (see also: Bacco and Van der Duin, 2010).
4 Be aware that the term 'contextual' with regard to ambidexterity means that every employee in an organization has to operate in an ambidextrous fashion. Contextual is here not meant in the sense of an organization adjusting its style of ambidexterity to the context in which it is operating.
5 The first part of this section is based on Chapter 10 of Trott et al. (2016).
6 See Delery and Doty (1996) for using these 'modes of theorizing' in the field of strategic human resource management.
7 A comparable concept can be found in economic science. The economist Nicholas Kaldor (1961) introduces the notion of 'stylized facts' (inspired by Jan Tinbergen's 'stylization') as a 'simplified imagination of an empirical fact' (Wikipedia). Doty and Glick (1994, p. 230) point out that typologies, if well developed, are more than classifications and "are complex theories that can be subjected to rigorous empirical testing".

4 The Theory of Contextual Innovation Management

4.1 Introduction: From Environment to Context

Determining the way innovation processes have to be adapted to the context requires a model that specifies the relationships between relevant aspects of the context and the innovation management in an effective and practical way. To do this, we describe the core concepts of a theory of contextual innovation management, how these concepts are related to each other (the structure), and how this theory can be operationalized.

Stating, reasoning, and even concluding that there is not a fixed set of best practices to innovate successfully and that every situation requires a different way of innovating is a first step in better understanding how innovation management takes place in organizations and to improve these practices and its outcomes (Dill, 1958; Hansen and Birkinshaw, 2007). A second step would be to build a theoretical framework that contains the factors that explain these differences in innovation management and shows how different contexts relate to different ways of innovation management. And a third step would be to turn this framework into an actionable process that enables innovation managers to apply the principles of contextual innovation management to their specific and ever-changing business situation (Reinmoeller and Van Baardwijk, 2005).

Organizations operate in a changing context (see: Emery and Trist, 1963) that simultaneously create 'situational opportunities' (e.g., changing consumer preferences, new technologies) and 'constraints' (e.g., strategic actions by competitors, new governmental legislation) (Johns, 2006, p. 386). The ratio of opportunities and limitations depends on the 'strategic power' to influence this environment and this power is in turn based on the strategic capabilities of the organization. The power of the organization to influence this balance is dialectical. If the ratio is towards more limitations than opportunities, the power of the organization is negatively influenced in the sense that the organization will be more occupied with trying to cope with the limitations than to profit from the existing opportunities. At the same time, hence the dialectics, the ratio is influenced by the power of organizations to limit the limitations and subsequently profit from the opportunities, thereby possibly becoming a very important, almost dominant player in the industry. Without presenting yet a fully comprehensive definition of context, we want to stress that to us context is more than the physical environment of an organization consisting of actors[1] but that it also includes factors (e.g., trends and developments) and institutional forces (Kalling, 2007; see also: Johns, 2006), such as regulations, norms, and standards. Thereby it comes rather close to the concept of an innovation system that strongly leans on system engineers and is defined "as a set of interrelated components working toward a common objective. Systems are made up of components, relationships, and attributes" (Carlsson et al., 2002, p. 234). Indeed, according to Adner (2006) companies should adjust their innovation strategies to their 'innovation ecosystem' since "(If) an innovation is a component of a larger solution that is itself under development, the innovation's success depends not only on its own successful completion but on the successful development and deployment of all other components of the system" (p. 2). Given that more often innovations can be characterized as system-innovations, the innovation-system has become a powerful determinant of innovation success, which makes context even more relevant.

The relationship of an organization with its context is an important aspect of a theory of contextual innovation management. Roughly, we distinguish between three perspectives on this relationship.

The first perspective is that a company considers itself as the central point of the context with its own ambitions and goals. The environment is more or less being shaped by the decisions and actions of the organizations. This can be regarded as 'inside-out thinking', prominent in the works of Gary Hamel and Prahalad and other management scholars and gurus who stress the importance of entrepreneurship (instead of good old-fashioned management). In this view, organizations should decide about their own fate, regardless of the context that they are in. Working hard will shape the context so it is not a limiting factor to the organization (anymore). These induced changes in the context enable the organization's plans for the future.

The second perspective sees things exactly the other way around. It views the organization as being influenced by its context so that the organization's first priority is to position itself in that context. The organization has to adapt itself to the environment, also known as 'environmental determinism' (Hrebiniak and Joyce, 1985). It can be considered as 'outside-in' thinking and is very much in line with the works of Michael Porter who regards the environment for organizations as given and advised organizations to position themselves as good as possible in an environment that cannot be determined or influenced by them. Porter's view is based on the structure-conduct-performance theory (Martin, 1989), which holds that the market or industry structure is given for every organization and that only by executing a specific kind of conduct (i.e., strategic behavior and actions) it can improve its performance relative to the performance of its competitors. The total profit or added value a market yields is fixed for all the organizations involved in that market and only by performing better than other organizations can an organization increase the share of this total profit.

The third perspective is, not surprisingly, in between the inside-out and outside-in perspectives. Basically, this view on the relation-organization context is that making a distinction between organization and context does not have much value since it is often difficult to see where the organization ends and the environment begins, and vice versa. The distinction or boundaries between an organization and its environment are often blurred and change constantly. In particular with regard to innovation we see the rise of 'open' approaches to management, such as the 'open innovation' paradigm of Henry Chesbrough (Chesbrough, 2003). The network approaches to innovation clearly contribute to this view on the relationships between organization and context where the innovation network can be considered a kind of 'intermediary' between the organization and the context. Also in approaches to 'networked innovation' (Van der Duin et al., 2014), several ways of organizing those relationships between the organization and its context can be distinguished (e.g., Ojasolo, 2008; Pisano and Verganti, 2008) such as distinguishing between the governance of an innovation network (hierarchical vs. flat) and the participation of organization (open vs. closed).

A note should be added: the three perspectives present the organization and context as separate entities, although in the third perspective this distinction is already becoming blurred. A dialectical approach to the study of organizations would mean that "(T)he conventional separation between organization and environment must be critically examined" (Benson, 1977, p. 9). Also, a dialectical approach criticizes a rational approach to organizational development and the rational-functional study of it, which is also responsible for this context-organization dichotomy. So, following the third perspective, the strategic choice ('inside-out') and environmental determinism do not have to be considered as mutual exclusive approaches, but can be seen as "independent perspectives that can be positioned on two separate continua to develop a typology of organizational adaptation" (Hrebiniak and Joyce, 1985, p. 336). In addition, it is considered to be essential that organizations are able to switch from strategy and organizational structure once the environment is changing. This leaves them with a paradox defined by Volberda (1996) where, in a situation of hyper-competition when more and more innovative organizations are operating, firms need to "reconcile the conflicting forces for change and stability" (Volberda, 1996, p. 360). Miller (1992a) frames this issue more in contingency terms by referring to the difficulty organizations have since they do not need only to fit their organization and strategy to the changing environment, but they also need to make sure that there is 'internal fit'. This means that organizations need to deal with internal organizational inconsistencies, such as a dynamic environment demanding quicker decision making and at the same time more involvement of highly trained specialists who "usually favor a slower, more analytical approach" (p. 159). Therefore, according to Volberda, the overall way to cope with these fast-changing environments that go beyond the control of any company is to develop sufficient strategic and organizational flexibility. We would like to add to this 'innovational flexibility' that, apart from creating a fit between the innovation management approaches to the context of an organization, also should enable an organization to adapt this approach once the environment is changing. Knowing the right contextual factors and the innovation management practices fitting these factors is one thing; being able to change the innovation management practice is another thing. Environments are dynamic and change ever more rapidly. Therefore, organizations should be resilient from an innovation perspective and need to master a diverse repertoire of innovation management practices to match the various possible environments (Reinmoeller and Van Baardwijk, 2005).

All three approaches assume that at a certain moment the environment is given for an organization but the way it relates to it differs. Whether an organization is able to choose its environment is not part of it, although we think that in the first approach the organization has the most degrees of freedom to decide in which context it wants to operate. Indeed, it might even be of great importance for organizations to have this choice because if an organization would not be able to make such a choice it could run into serious strategic troubles if it fails to influence its environment and at the same time is not able to choose a different environment in which to compete. Therefore, the theory of contextual innovation management is based on and perhaps only possible if two assumptions are met:

1. Organizations cannot influence their environment but have to adapt themselves to it and are able to do that.
2. Organizations are able to decide in which environment they want to compete.

The second assumption of course holds another assumption, namely that an organization has sufficient 'strategic degrees of freedom' that enable it to move from one context to another. Moreover, just as with any other type of freedom (e.g., freedom of religion) this freedom is not unlimited since it cannot be expected that an organization can easily or without any limitations shift its business activities to a completely different industry. Chances are pretty low that a company operating in a fast-moving consumer good industry will leave that industry to take its chances in the offshore petrochemical industry (and don't have any problems in realizing that). Nevertheless, some companies do move to different industries and have reinvented themselves throughout their business history (famous examples are Shell and Nokia). Moreover, often innovations come from other industries, known as 'cross-overs', which shows that it is indeed possible for a company to not only change its business background (e.g., organizational culture, mission) but also to shift to other industries and gain business success there as well.

Stating that organizations relate in a particular way to their environment needs some nuance since it assumes that organizations are homogenous entities that as a whole relate to their environment. In reality, many (large) organizations consist of several departments involved in different business activities performing in different environments. This means that each sub-department manages its innovations activities differently because the different (sub-)environments put different demands on them. To meet those specific demands a sub-department needs to have the 'organizational freedom' to make its (own) decisions on how to manage its innovation processes. This brings us to assumption 3 for applying contextual innovation management:

3.   An organization or its (sub-)departments (or business units) can decide by themselves how to organize their innovation processes.

A centralized organization will leave no room for a contextual approach to innovation management because of its top-down nature. A centralized organization will have one way ('the corporate style') of managing the organization's innovation processes to which every innovation manager should adhere. This results in a set of best practices that will be applied in every part of the organization, thereby very much resembling the situation described in the Chapter 2 about best practices or success factors for organizations. Of course, it is possible that the corporate innovation management center ('headquarters') decides to give every innovation department in every sub-department the freedom to make its own decisions. However, that would turn the centralized organization into a decentralized one with regard to innovation. If other company functions such as finance, human resource management, and marketing, which are important to managing innovation, would remain centralized then the innovation sub-departments would end up with a rather ineffective mix of centralized and decentralized organizational arrangements. For instance, innovation managers might have decision power to make their own necessary external contacts required for innovation or choose their own type of innovation process. But they would not have the freedom to acquire the people with the required skills since that would still be a matter that is decided upon by the central office for human resources. This leads to the fourth assumption:

4.   An organizational unit needs to have sufficient degrees of freedom to make their own decision regarding organizational structure in general and innovation in particular.

As Pennings (1987, p. 224) puts it: "contingency approaches allow a certain degree of freedom in selecting or modifying a particular structure". In addition, more generally, Romme (2017) sees a big future of decentralized management that "explicitly draws on principles of distributed intelligence" (p. 6).

These four assumptions of the theory of contextual innovation management focus on the organization that carries out contextualized innovation process. However, since this theory also takes context into account we add two assumptions to this theory that focus on context.

5. The context of an organization needs to be sufficiently stable for at least the development time of an innovation.
6. The context of an organization is sufficiently diverse to warrant contextual innovation management.

We would like to note that assumptions 5 and 6 are to a certain extent contrary to each other. Assumption 5 stresses that at least a certain stability of the context is required to make a formal and explicit approach to innovation management possible. If contexts would change constantly and drastically, it becomes impossible for organizations to develop and implement contextualized innovation processes. On the other hand, if a context would be completely stable and have no variety then there would be no point of applying contextual innovation management since there is no reason to diversify the innovation processes to fit the context. We make a distinction between diversity and variety. With diversity we mean that there are multiple contexts, as expressed by multiple contextual factors, to which an organization should adjust its innovation process. This diversity can be fueled by the changing context itself but also because the organization chooses to operate at the same time in a different context (see also assumption 2). Variety relates to a change in context over time.[2] It is exactly these two types of changes (in choosing a different context and changing contexts) that make sticking to a fixed set of innovation-related success factors a recipe for business disaster.

4.2 Contextual Factors: The Core of a Theory of Contextual Innovation Management

Organizations operate in a context that provides opportunities for them and at the same time constrains them. To *contextualize* innovation management and build a theory of contextual innovation management requires that we look at the context of an organization from an innovation perspective in general and from a *contextual* innovation management perspective in particular. For that we need to distinguish between various so-called *contextual factors*. These factors can be regarded as specific characteristics of the context in which an organization operates and that are relevant for deciding how to organize the organization's innovation processes. Some of these contextual factors might directly be related to the organization's environment or industry but some do not and that is why we use the term context instead of environment or industry. In this section, we discuss three contextual factors that are often found in literature:[3] industry, organization, and technology. By discussing these contextual factors we are of course aware that we have left out other possible contextual factors, such as leadership (De Jong and Den Hartog, 2007), availability of slack resources or presence of an effective capital application procedure (Kalling, 2007), a firm's ecosystem and the level of formalization of the innovation process itself (Salerno et al., 2015), and 'entrepreneurial power and capabilities' (Khurum et al., 2015).[4]

It is important to note that we assume that contextual factors cannot be controlled by those who manage the innovation process. The nature of the industry, the type of organization within which the innovation process is completed, and the state of the technology that is applied in the innovation process are assumed to be beyond the control of the manager involved with adapting the innovation process to the context. Contextual factors differ for R&D and innovation managers because the environment for the innovation processes can differ and because the factors that they can and cannot control do differ. The three contextual factors that we will discuss next—type of industry, type of organization, and type of technology—are typical examples of contextual factors.

Industry

Industry contains the market as a whole, including users (and their preferences), suppliers, competitors, industry-specific regulations or institutions, business models, and customs. For instance, in the pharmaceutical industry innovation processes are heavily regulated while in some software industries producers of software have much room for experimentation with new software. On the other hand, different industries can have different competition structures. The dynamics ('heartbeat') of industries can change. This heartbeat is often determined by the time-to-market of new products and services or the duration of the life cycle or the speed of diffusion of new products and services. The environment or context, as discussed in section 4.1, is close to industry but it is not exactly the same because environment is a broader concept including stakeholders and societal 'forces' as well.

It is important to note that industries are not static and it is not always easy to decide where one industry ends and another starts. The boundaries of industries can become very fluid due to changes in preferences of customers, new regulations, and especially because of new technologies. The dynamic times in which we currently live and in which companies are competing with each other even raises the question whether there still exists industries. The structure of our economy and its capitalist order is changing constantly. Just as we see established companies going bankrupt in no time and new companies (such as Uber and Airbnb) rise extremely fast, so are old industries disappearing and new industries emerging. Nevertheless, industry as a concept is still vital and widely used, and can have an important influence on how organizations manage their innovation processes.

Looking from another angle, other industries can influence a particular industry. Not only by competing with it, but also by being inspired by it. Technology and innovation are a common means to relate industries with each other. 'General purpose technologies' (see: Lipsey et al., 2005), as they are being called, such as electricity and the internet, have specific and valuable applications in every industry. Such general purpose technologies do change the way of working and the way innovation processes are completed, in many industries. Cross-innovations, another example, are innovations that have been applied in one industry and are then used in a different industry. It is also possible that industries merge. A good example is the merger between the telecommunications industry, the media industry, and the information industry. What would you consider a smart phone? A telecommunication, a media, or an information technology product? And, is it a product (innovation) or a service (innovation)?

Changes within and between industries affect the way companies innovate. The development of a general purpose technology could result in an innovation process dominated by technology. And the merger or confluence of two industries could mean that a company can't innovate by itself anymore and is, more or less, being forced to adapt to 'open-innovation' practices. These developments make the management of innovation not only more relevant and interesting, but also more difficult. A telecommunication company that decides to work together with an information technology company to develop a new product or service will be confronted with a rather different way of innovating. For instance, a telecommunication company is used to extensively test possible new products and services, thereby putting emphasis on quality, whereas an IT company cares much more about speed to market and would put the first version of a new product or service into the market as soon as possible to receive feedback and improve the innovation (Berkhout and Van der Duin, 2007). Things can become even more complicated as two divisions of a company operate in different industries. The *corporate* innovation will then have a hell of a job to make sure that both divisions are able to apply their own way of innovation management tailored to their specific industry, while at the same time coordinating both innovation practices to prevent wasting valuable company's resources (Van den Elst et al., 2006).

The industry in which a company operates is that part of the (physical) context of the environment that is closest to the organization. It is their immediate 'space of competition', where their most important stakeholders reside (i.e., customers), where they collect the resources they need for their production processes (i.e., from their suppliers), and in which also the most relevant legal boundaries and standards are set. However, as said earlier, at the same it is wise to not take the industry for granted and forever. Especially for innovation it is crucial to go beyond the own industry. That is, an industry refers to the actual collection of businesses of which the company is part of. When companies need to redefine their business to stay in 'business', they need to search a new business. For instance, an oil company is in the oil business. But with regard to innovation, and in addressing the strategic issue of what will their business be in the future, it is better for the oil company to consider itself in the 'industry' of 'energy'. In that way, the 'oil' company is able to redefine itself and its business and make sure that it keeps addressing its ultimate mission: providing its customers and companies with energy. That might be oil in the present, but something else in the future, such as gas, solar power, or nuclear energy. The energy business is also interesting because it shows how its dynamics, speed of change, or 'heartbeat' can change. In former times, the time horizon of this industry was measured in decades, but now with the arrival of alternative energy sources such as solar power and wind energy this time horizon has shortened drastically, thereby impacting the innovation process severely.[5]

Box 4.1   Market

Although the market is a part of industry (see previously), we consider the market sufficiently relevant and distinct to devote a few words to it since it is considered an important factor in many studies on contingency and contextual approaches to innovation management. The market is the place where eventually the innovation is being bought and since that ultimately defines the success of the innovation and its underlying innovation process, the market and its characteristics are factors that managers of innovation processes should take into account.

Lu and Chang (2002) specifically study how R&D and marketing can be integrated into new product development (NPD) processes. They conclude that factors such as "role flexibility, joint reward, values integration of top, job rotation, and interaction between functional leaders in NPD teams" contribute to integration (p. 162). Another market-related contingency study is by Pasche and Magnusson (2013), who research how various product platforms can be related to modules in NPD. They identify factors such as the amount of demand for product customization, margin, and market share to determine different types of modularization and product platforms that impact the type of organization and the way it works. Market is not only a contingency factor in itself, but Kok and Biemans (2009) distinguish within a 'market-oriented product innovation process' contingency factors such as 'the objectives of change programs', 'patterns of change', and 'approaches to change', each of which differ according to whether a firm is low-tech or high-tech. High-tech and low-tech companies operate in different industrial contexts (i.e., the knowledge level and preferences of customers are different, the pace of technological change is different).

Organization[6]

Innovation management takes place within and/or between organizations, which makes it a relevant contextual factor.[7] For instance, Van de Woestyne et al. (2007) develop three archetypes of innovative organizations based on how they deal with strategic issues such as flexibility, efficiency, balance, and organizational structure (centralized vs. decentralized). Blindenbach-Driessen and Van den Ende (2006) have investigated 'innovation in project-based firms'[8] and find relevant factors such as 'explicit project selection', senior management support', and 'the availability of sufficient experts' (p. 556).

Organization is a very broad topic and actually the most classical *contingency* factor (see also Chapter 3). With regard to the relationship between organizational structure and innovation, we refer here to Trott (Trott, 2008, p. 92) who makes, based on Burns and Stalker (1961; see also Chapter 3), a distinction between organic and mechanistic organizational structures in which the following elements play a role:

- Formal versus informal channels of communication;
- Mechanic versus organic organizational structure;
- Loose and informal versus strict and formal control;
- Flexible on-job behavior/constrained on job-behavior.

We assume that the connotation of the terms organic and mechanistic and their acquaintance enables the reader to fill in themselves the values of the elements. For now, we want to emphasize that the mechanistic organizational structure is not completely in line with the level of freedom contextual innovation management requires (see in particular assumptions 2, 3, and 4). In particular, formal channels of communication, mechanistic organizational structures, strict and formal control, and constrained job behaviour might make the implementation of contextual innovation management rather diffi-cult. On the other hand, we should note that the formality of the mechanical structured organization can also be a contributing factor to implementing contextual innovation management (see also Chap-ter 6, section 6.1).

Technology

Technology is an important ingredient of innovation as well as an important driver for innovation processes, resulting in many different technological trajectories (e.g., Pavitt, 1984). Nowadays, innovation is considered to be more than just *technological* innovation, but no doubt we can state that often technological developments provide the set of opportunities that fuel innovation. The specific innovation that ulti-mately becomes truly successful, meaning that it follows a diffusion curve and thereby gets beyond the introductory stage, is often decided upon by non-technological factors, such as decisions about marketing and busi-ness models. We therefore consider management of innovation also a broader concept as management of *technology*.[9]

Indeed, many authors have stressed the importance of taking tech-nology into account as an important factor in managing innovation. For instance, Tushman and Rosenkopf (1992) have described technol-ogy development as a technology life cycle, influenced by evolutionary socio-cultural processes in which technological discontinuities through dominant designs leads to incremental improvements. In addition, Aber-nathy (1978) states that the amount of process innovation in an industry increases after the establishment of dominant designs. Dominant designs are the designs that emerge after radical innovations are created. As a result Abernathy (1978) claims that radical product innovations pre-cede process innovations. Furthermore, Abernathy and Clark (1985) put forward that different types of innovation link to different patterns of technological evolution and, subsequently, to different managerial envi-ronments, thereby emphasizing the difference between innovations that disrupt certain organizational competences and those that refine and improve them. Tushman and Anderson (1986) state that technological discontinuities can have an impact on organizational competences and that they increase environmental uncertainty and munificence.

From a contingency perspective, Drejer (2002) asserts that we should move beyond the distinction between Schumpeterian 'creative destruc-tion' and technology exploitation, and therefore he defines three 'situa-tions' for innovation management: 1) exploiting of existing technologies; 2) stable technological change; and 3) disruptive technological change (p. 10). More specifically: in a 'technology exploiting' situation the inno-vation process is (should be) formalized, documented, and linear (p. 12); in a 'sustainable technology change' situation it is (should be) formalized but not a stage-gate model, and the focus is on the procedure (p. 14);

and in a 'disruptive technology change' situation the innovation process is "an implicit activity in the thinking of a very small number of key individuals applying and building tacit knowledge and experiences in the process" (p. 15).

With regard to technological trajectories, a more qualitative approach to technology development than the quantitative view in terms of high tech or low tech is suggested by Souitaris (2000), who based on Pavitt's (1984) taxonomy, finds different determinants for innovation, such as acquisition of information, technology strategy, training and incentives to employees, and customer feedback.

Some authors do refer to 'type of innovation' as a contextual factor that is related to 'type of technology'. Some remarks regarding type of innovation can be found in Box 4.2.

Box 4.2   Innovation

This contextual factor does not entail the innovation *process* but only the innovation itself. Otherwise, the dependent variable and the independent variable are being mixed, causing conceptual and theoretical problems (see, for instance, Salerno et al., 2015, who in building a typology of innovation processes also take aspects of the innovation processes itself into account and not just external variables or contextual factors that explain the variation in innovation processes).

An innovation can simply be defined as the outcome of an innovation process (Drejer, 2002, p. 6). This seems to suggest that the way an innovation process has developed and is managed is not particularly relevant since the innovation process has ended with its implementation. But although the specific form of the innovation in terms of, for instance, price, technology used, or shape, will be difficult to decide upfront (after all, it is an innovation and therefore rather unpredictable at the beginning), innovation managers do decide at the start of their 'innovation journey' what their ambition level is. That is, they have to formulate upfront if they aim to develop an incremental innovation or go for a radical innovation, which obviously influences the type of innovation process. The type of innovation is therefore seen as a contextual factor.

So, one way to distinguish between different types of innovation is to look at the impact they have on business and society. Innovations that have a great impact on the way we live (personally), on society, and on how we do business are called radical innovations or transformational innovations. Examples are the steam-engine, the telephone, the automobile, and the Internet. At the other end of this continuum, we have incremental innovations that only display a slight change with the former version of the same innovation. New product releases or software updates are examples of these types of innovations.

Other types of innovation emphasize qualitative differences instead of quantitative differences in terms of impact. For instance, one can distinguish between product, service, business model, and organizational innovations. These types of innovations can be of course radical or incremental, so that both types of innovation relate to each other orthogonally. But in general, innovation processes to create new services are different from those that are meant to create new products and hence type of innovation is a contextual factor (Hipp and Grupp, 2005).

In conclusion, we have discussed three common contextual factors. These factors are assumed to be out of the control of innovation or R&D managers that shape innovation processes, yet these factors are claimed to have a significant effect on the way these innovation processes are managed. The main types of contextual factors can differ for such managers and hence more factors are discussed in the literature, one of which is 'degree of uncertainty'. This is a generic and overarching factor.

Box 4.3   Uncertainty

Although uncertainty is often mentioned in contingency and contextual studies, we do not consider it a singular contextual factor since it can be viewed as 'classification' of a contextual factor, such as uncertainty (high/low) of a market, or uncertainty (high/low) of a technology. Nevertheless, because it so often appears in contingency and contextual studies, we want to devote a few words on it in this box. Especially since uncertainty is a very relevant feature of innovation processes, both with regard to its process and to the innovation itself in terms of rate of adoption and for which goal it is being used. Classical studies on contingency have addressed this factor (Shenhar, 2001). Indeed, Shenhar (2001) himself develops a framework that classifies projects ('temporary organizations *within* organizations', according to Shenhar) into four levels of *technological* uncertainty (low, medium, high, and super high). Lynn and Akgün (1998) focus not only on technology uncertainty (TU) but also on *market* uncertainty (MU) which results in a 2 by 2 matrix in which four innovation strategies can be distinguished: learning or market-based innovation (high MU/low TU), learning-based innovation (high MU/High TU), process and quantitative-based innovation (low MU/low TU), and learning-, technology- and speed-based innovation (low MU/high TU).

Tidd (2001) considers uncertainty (and complexity) as 'key environmental contingencies' for innovation management. By distinguishing between high and low uncertainty (of the environment of the innovating organization), and between high and low complexity (i.e., the number of technologies and their interactions), four specific organizational structures and processes to manage innovation are distinguished (low U/Low C: differentiated; high Y, low C: innovative; high U/high C: complex; low U/high U: networked).

Describing the contextual factors separately does not mean that they operate in isolation or that are not connected to each other. The different contexts in which innovation management is applied in different ways and is constituted by different combinations of the contextual factors. For instance, Balachandra and Friar (1997) build a 'contingency cube' for new product development that consists of three factors: technology (high vs. low), innovation (incremental vs. radical), and market (existing vs. new). And Jin et al. (1997) develop a typology of NPD-processes consisting of six contextual factors or 'dimensions' that are relevant in the relationship between an effective NPD process and its context, such as product uncertainty, the ability to accelerate the NPD process, product complexity, and the seniority of the product champion.

4.3 The Structure of a Theory of Contextual Innovation Management

Having a theory on contextual innovation management means that the various contextual factors can be related to various types of innovation management in a structured and validated manner. In section 4.2, we described three contextual factors. Before we explore how they relate to innovation management, we briefly discuss the concept of innovation management. In Chapter 1, we defined innovation management as the governance and organization of the innovation process as a project. Another definition comes from Drejer (2002, p. 4): "innovation management, understood as being the activities that firms undertake in order to yield new solutions within products, production and administration". Innovation can be addressed at different levels. Ranging from the macro-level where scholars study the innovative character of a country (i.e., national economy) and national innovation policies, through the level of innovation systems and networks, innovation within industries, innovation management on corporate level and its accompanying innovation processes, and the innovation qualities of employees (such as the phenomenon of 'product champions'). In the discussion of contextual factors in section 4.2, we also referred to studies that were looking at practices and principles of new product development (NPD).[10]

In this book, we focus on innovation management at the level of the organization (profit or non-profit) in combination with the level of innovation processes. That is, we address a specific innovation process aimed at developing and implementing a specific innovation. In addition, sometimes we address how organizations, at a corporate level, at a divisional, or on a team level (depending on the level of organizational centralism) manage innovation processes. Although NPD and (corporate) innovation management refer to different levels of analysis, they are closely connected and that is why we take them together. Within a single organization different innovation processes can coexist, which is in line with a contextual approach to innovation and required for an ambidextrous organization (Salerno et al., 2015, p. 61). Nevertheless, a coordination of corporate innovation management and NPD processes is also required for establishing internal consistency, preventing organizations from waste scarce company resources thereby lowering their organizational efficiency and effectiveness.

In Chapter 1, we distinguished between four different *generations* of innovation management. Since apparently the principles of innovation management of these generations are still being used, even sometimes within one and the same organization, we can discard the historical character of these generations. Nowadays, organizations can consider these 'generations' as a contemporary set of ways or styles to innovate from which to choose, and of course, this choice should be dependent on the relevant contextual factors.

A theory of contextual innovation management asserts that an organization increases its innovative performance if it matches the different ways of managing innovation processes and relevant contextual factors. The success or performance of innovation management, therefore, has to be measured. Since that can be done in many ways, we have to make a choice. Since we have defined innovation as the outcome of an innovation process, we are especially interested in the output of an innovation process. This does not mean that the input and throughput phase of an innovation process are unimportant. At least they are important assumptions for having a good output phase of an innovation process. However, for a direct measurement of the innovative performance of an organization we need to look at how well it does in putting new products and services into the market and how well these innovations diffuse through the market. Possibly relevant for measuring innovation performance are: number of innovation processes completed, amount of innovations introduced in a certain period, and amount products and services sold or market share obtained with them. Notice that these measurements are innovation related and thereby more specific than measurements such as growth of turnover and profit, which are more relevant when measuring overall organizational performance.[11]

To develop a theory of contextual innovation management we connect the contextual factors we described in section 4.2 with the different ways of innovation management described in Chapter 1. Figure 4.1 illustrates this connection. The contextual factors are the independent variable (i.e., the explaining factors) and the different ways of innovation management are the dependent variables (i.e., what is to be explained):

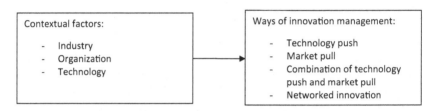

Figure 4.1 The Contextual Factors and the Different Ways of Innovation Management

Figure 4.1 shows the basic model of contextual innovation management. The contextual factors determine the way of innovating. To put it in a more contingent or contextual way, the way of innovation management has to adapt to or to fit the contextual factors. However, this model might be considered too simple since the idea is that by choosing the right contextual factors and having the way of innovation adjusted to it, the organization becomes more innovative and improves its innovation performance. Figure 4.2 shows a modified model:

Figure 4.2 The Contextual Factors, the Ways of Innovation Management, and the Innovation Performance

In addition, Figure 4.2 leaves room for improvement since it gives a static and one-directional picture of how these three elements are influencing each other. Contextual innovation management should not be a static theory since the practice it attempts to describe is not static. Contingent and contextual factors are by nature not constant. Not only do their values change over time, the set of relevant contextual factors is not constant either (Donaldson, 1987). Tidd (2001, p. 174) provides us with a more realistic model by linking the three elements dynamically and adding the element of innovation:

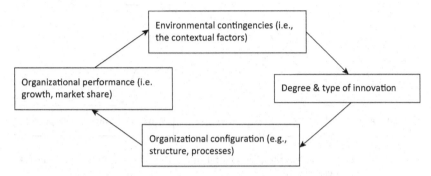

Figure 4.3 Innovation, Environment, and Performance (Tidd, 2001, p. 174)

An important aspect of Figure 4.3 is that it has a feedback loop starting at environmental contingencies, via degree and type of innovation, organizational configuration, and organizational performance, going back to environmental contingencies. This feedback loop gives the theory of contextual innovation management the dynamics it tries to capture. Furthermore, it indicates that it is not only the context that determines the organizational performance, but that the performance also affects the environment (context) of an organization. This is very much in line with the third approach to the relationship between context and organization as described in section 4.2, and which holds probably for most organizations. It also is in line with the notion that by developing innovations an organization also innovates itself, as well the context in which it operates. In addition, Gebhardt (2005, p. 21) states that: "innovativeness is perceived as the best structural fit to an ever-changing environment". An organization not only optimizes its innovation management by adjusting it to contextual factors, but innovativeness itself contributes to a structural fit of the whole organization to a changing context, thereby illustrating the cyclic nature of context, innovation management, and innovation performance (see the following and Figure 4.4).

We do need to make, however, three adjustments to the model of Tidd. The first one is that we consider the innovation itself (i.e., ranging from incremental to radical) as a contextual factor and thereby part of Tidd's 'environmental contingencies' (see also Box 4.2). Secondly, we focus on innovation performance, i.e., the innovativeness of an organization, and not on 'organizational performance', since that concept is too broad for the goal and focus of a theory of contextual innovation management. Moreover, organizational performance is not wholly determined by innovation performance. Thirdly, we focus on innovation management and not on 'organizational configuration', since that concept is, once again, too broad for the goal and focus of a theory of contextual innovation management. Based on this the model in Figure 4.4 results.

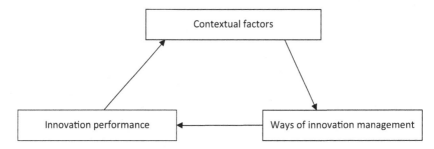

Figure 4.4 Contextual Factors, Ways of Innovation Management, and Innovation Performance

The next question is then, of course: how do the contextual factors and the ways of innovation management relate? In principle, given the amount of both type of variables, the connections can be numerous. This would endanger very much the practical qualities of the theory and its model. In Chapter 3 and section 4.2, we described contextual approaches to innovation management. From these approaches, we can make the following list of relationships. The next step is (once again) to make the assumptions of the model explicit. As can be noted from section 4.1, we assume the following:

1. Organizations cannot influence their environment but have to adapt themselves to it and be able to do so. (Of course, adaptation is easier to an environment that a company can choose itself).
2. Organizations are able to decide in which environment they want to compete.
3. An organization or its (sub-)departments (or business units) can decide by themselves how to organize their innovation processes.
4. An organizational unit needs to have sufficient degrees of freedom to make their own decision regarding organizational structure in general and innovation in particular.
5. The context of an organization needs to be sufficiently stable for at least the development time of an innovation.
6. The context of an organization is sufficiently diverse to warrant contextual innovation management.

For now, we would like to add two assumptions:

7. An organization has in its mission 'to be, to stay, or to become innovative', or similar wordings, as its core elements. Innovation has to

be sufficiently important to an organization to develop its 'own' way of innovating.[12]
8.   The success of innovation can be measured sufficiently specific.

With these assumptions it is also possible to determine where the contextual innovation management can be applied and where it cannot. Since the latter can be regarded as the test of whether this theory is scientific or not and where it is valid or not, it becomes clear how this theory can be falsified.

To sum up, for determining the structure of a theory of contextual innovation management we have described its:[13]

- main contextual factors (see section 4.2);
- a model that links the contextual factors with the various ways of innovation management and innovation performance;
- the concept of innovation management;
- the different ways of innovation management (see also Chapter 1, in particular section 1.3);
- eight assumptions that define when and where the theory should be applied, is valid, and for what it should be used.

4.4 Concluding Remarks

The way an organization relates to its environment is one of the most important questions for both managers and management scientists. Just as in psychology the state of mind of a person is not all explained by her inner state, so it the functioning and the degree of success of an organization not only dependent on its own decisions and actions. All organizations, regardless of size, operate in a social and economic context that has a major impact on that organization. That does not mean that they depend on the context; the context also offers opportunities and is also influenced by organizations, certainly if they have a certain size.

In the context of contextual innovation management, the context of organizations consists of several (contextual) factors that form an important guideline for organizing innovation processes. The following contextual factors are distinguished: industry, market, innovation, organization, and technology. These factors offer many benefits to innovative organizations such as providing structure to a context that is increasingly complex and uncertain. Also, they provide clear guidelines of how to organize the innovation process that fits with the context. The idea behind contextual innovation management is therefore that the relevant contextual factors determine how the innovation process (or processes) should be managed in such a way that the innovation performance becomes high.

It is important that the innovative organizations have sufficient space and knowledge to adjust their innovation processes to the factors in the context. Moreover, it is essential that the correct contextual factors are being taken as the starting point for shaping the innovation processes. In the search for the right factors, a good mix of internal and external expertise must be sought. The contextual factors found must be a correct representation of the changes in the context of the innovative organization. After all, a contextual approach to the existing innovation process means that it will be changed and that it is expanded with multiple innovation processes. Contextual innovation processes are therefore new innovation processes. Contextual innovation management, it has been said before, is an innovation of the innovation process. Since innovation always relates to the future, that is why changes must be made, contextual factors must always have a future character. The changes that are taking place in the context are expressed in various contextual factors.

Notes

1 For a study how 'business innovation modes' can differ across countries and regions, i.e., a physical context/environment, see: Parrilli and Heras, 2016.
2 Indeed, if the contextual factors change over time so much, one could argue whether we are still talking about the same context.
3 In section 3.5 we already discussed four contextual innovation management studies in which these factors were present. See for an extensive overview of contingency factors with respect to technological innovation: Souitaris, 1999.
4 Sometimes even certain contextual or contingency factors are not significant. For instance, Van Echtelt et al. (2007) find in their study on supplier involvement no indications that these differ whether they are dealing with highly or less innovative projects.
5 See Minderhoud and Fraser (2005) for a study on how shorter life cycles and a more rapid pace of technology development in consumer electronics industry influences the management of product development.
6 Be aware that we are talking here about the organization itself, the organizational structure to say. It is not about the organization of the contextualized innovation process.
7 For an example of how organizations in general can develop in different circumstances, see Van de Ven and Poole (1995) who distinguish between four different processes of change in organizations: life cycle, teleology, dialectics, and evolution.
8 Given the crucial differences between projects and innovation processes, this seems to us like a contradiction-in-terms.
9 See Drejer (1996) for an overview of frameworks of management of technologies thereby adopting a 'contingent approach'.
10 For an overview of NPD frameworks, see: Shepherd and Ahmed, 2000.
11 Section 6.4 deals with this topic more extensively.
12 Please bear in mind that organizations should seriously consider the question whether to innovate or not to innovate. After all, development of an entirely new product/service is a strategy that is highly risky and mostly takes a long time to generate return on investment. In situations where quick reactions are required—for example because turn-over or profits are shrinking quickly—cost-cutting may be a more viable strategy than innovation, because its returns are more certain and will emerge sooner. So, depending on the

context, alternative strategies other than starting an innovation process should be considered. In particular, adopting an innovation strategy can be compared to alternative strategies such as:

- Improving an existing product/service rather than developing a fully new product/service.
- Improving the process of working (supply, production, distribution, and marketing) rather than the product/service.
- Expanding the market with the same products/service.
- Cutting costs in the existing organization.
- Buying another organization with a product portfolio rather than developing the products.

13 Drazin and Van de Ven (1985, p. 514) refer to Dubin (1976) who states that "every theory is a contingency theory", and that for a law of interaction to hold, assumptions must be made about starting premises, boundaries, and systems states. Boundary conditions specify the ranges over which a relationship is expected to hold, and system states specify the temporal period and other conditions under which the relationships hypothesized are expected to occur. Drazin and Van de Ven, 1985, p. 514)

5 A Process for Contextual Innovation Management

5.1 Introduction

To carry out contextual innovation management a process is required. In this chapter, we describe seven steps plan by which an organization can apply the principles of contextual innovation as outlined in Chapters 3 and 4 to its own specific situation. The process is of course generic which means that, in principle, it can be applied by every organization. But, as the theory of contextual innovation requires, the outcomes of this process, that is, the contextual factors and the corresponding contextualized innovation processes, might be different for each organization.

5.2 The Operationalization of Contextual Innovation Management

Operationalizing contextual innovation management is divided in seven steps: the first two steps create a vison on the company's context that has an effect on innovation processes, the next three steps develop the company's general contextual innovation approach, and the last two steps apply the approach to a specific innovation process.

Create a vision on the company's context:

1. Select the most important contextual factors for innovation processes in the company.
2. Choose key aspects and relevant values for each of the selected contextual factors.

Develop the company's general contextual innovation approach:

3. Create a scheme reflecting the possible combinations of contextual factors.
4. Determine the degrees of freedom in adapting innovation processes to the context.
5. Design specific innovation processes for each possible context.

Apply the approach to a specific innovation process:

6. Assess the values on the relevant contextual factors for a specific innovation project.
7. Select the accompanying innovation process as a starting point.

The first two steps are about creating a vision on the relevant context for innovation processes in the company. In step 1, the most important contextual factors for innovation processes in the company are formulated. Examples of contextual factors are 'type of industry', 'type of organization', and 'type of technology (see section 4.2). In step 2, for each of the selected contextual factors, a key aspect is chosen as operationalization of that factor and a limited number of possible values for that aspect are formulated. For example, the contextual factor 'the type of technology' can be operationalized in terms of degree of newness. Degree of newness can have two alternative values: 'incrementally new technology' and 'radically new technology'.

The next three steps are about developing the company's general contextual innovation approach. In step 3, the alternative values of the most important contextual factors need to be combined in a scheme. This scheme can be one-dimensional in situations with one most important factor or it can be two- or three-dimensional when two or three factors are most important. The scheme reflects possible combinations of contextual factors for the company. In step 4, possible adaptations in the innovation process are explored. Possible adaptations are the degrees of freedom that innovation and R&D managers can use to adapt the innovation process. For example, the structure of the innovation process can be changed by creating phases in the process that, in turn, can be completed sequentially or in parallel. In step 5, the relevant contextual factors (from step 3) and the degrees of freedom to adapt the innovation process (from step 4) are combined. In this fifth step, for all relevant combinations of contextual factors different types of innovation processes are created. This step thus creates the menu from which R&D and innovation managers can select a particular way to manage an innovation process. This means that a set of pre-specified innovation processes is created, each of which is applicable in a specific situation (depending on the values for the contextual factors).

The final two steps apply the contextual innovation approach to a specific innovation process. The actual application of contextual innovation management for an innovation process involves two additional steps. In step 6, the values for the most important contextual factors should be determined for the particular innovation process. For example, the goal can be to use a radically new technology in a turbulent industry. In step 7, the innovation process envisioned for the particular combination of factors should be selected. This process then represents a starting point for the design and planning of an innovation process that fits its context. In the case of a radically new technology, for example, the innovation process is designed and planned in a completely different way than in the case of applying an incrementally new technology (see also: Verloop, 2006).

The seven steps to operationalize contextual innovation management will be described in more detail in the following three subsections.

5.3 Creating a Vision on the Company's Context

Vision formation for contextual innovation management means that a company explores the relevant alternative types of contexts for its innovation processes. It is divided into two steps.

Step 1: Selecting Most Important Contextual Factors for Innovation Processes in the Company

In section 4.2 we described three contextual factors: industry, organization, and technology. This list is not exhaustive but it covers a variety of contextual factors. From this list, a subset of one, two or all three contextual factors needs to be selected. These factors, in turn, can be operationalized in terms of specific aspects that fit the particular context of a company.

The selection of contextual factors can be done in various ways. Innovation managers, product managers, and industry experts can be requested to indicate which of the factors has a prominent effect on the adaptation of innovation processes. If, for example, a company operates in one industry only, this industry is given and hence the effect of different industries on innovation processes need not to be taken into account in the day-to-day practice of adapting innovation processes completed by that company. In the pharmaceutical industry, for example, medicines used to be developed in a highly regulated and prescribed way. Medicine development was based on systematic creation and testing of chemical substances in a chemical laboratory. The stages of such an innovation process were determined by regulation, demanding subsequent phases of clinical testing. Obviously, in this example the type of industry has a tremendous effect on the way innovation processes are managed. However, if the company remains active in just that industry, then adaptation of different innovation processes to the contextual factor industry is not required. To put it differently, the contextual factor industry is a 'dormant' contextual factor that is not important in the day-to-day adaptation of innovation processes of a pharmaceutical company to the context. However, once new technologies and disciplines enter the industry, this so-called 'dormant' contextual factor 'type of industry' becomes important again. This was the case when biochemical start-ups began to disrupt the pharmaceutical industry with medicines that were adapted to the genetic characteristics of the patient, such as with cancer medicines (like Herceptin) that were adapted to genetically originating types of cancer. Some types of breast cancer are based on a patient's genetic material, and that can be tested using a diagnostic instrument, after which the doctor can decide about the best mix of treatments. Pharmaceutical companies missed the expertise to develop such medicines and accompanying diagnostic technologies and hence aligned with academic spin-offs and biochemical start-ups. This fundamental change in the industry had its effect on the structure and type of innovation process. Innovation processes were completed by alliances of companies with complementary knowledge and competences. The systematic creation and selection process of chemical substances became replaced by a process containing a fundamental diagnosis of the cause of a disease and the design and development of molecules representing a remedy for that disease while not affecting the individual's health in other ways.

A similar situation may occur if all innovation processes are planned within the boundaries of one company (organization). In that case the contextual factor 'company' (organization) remains the same and does not affect the day-to-day innovation processes. The factor 'company' is a so-called dormant contextual factor that, only if changes appear in the organization, may significantly affect innovation processes. For example, over time the company may have to go through fundamental reorganizations or may be bought by another company (see section 5.2), all of which may also require fundamental changes in the innovation process. This means that changes in the organization require changes in the innovation process. In some cases, major corporations consist of business units that can be considered completely different companies in terms of how they are organized and managed and hence how innovation processes should be managed.

Therefore, some of the contextual factors may be less important for the day-to-day adaptation of ongoing innovation processes and hence a selection of contextual factors can be determined. It is important to keep on looking at 'dormant contextual factors' and whether changes do require a reconsideration of their role. Disruptions or fundamental changes in the context may make such dormant contextual factors highly relevant again.

Step 2: Choosing Key Aspects and Relevant Values for Each of the Selected Contextual Factors

Each of the contextual factors in fact comprises a category of (sub-)factors or aspects. The contextual factor 'type of organization', for example, may refer to a host of different aspects that have an impact on innovation processes, such as the degree of hierarchy in the organization. A high degree of hierarchy in the organization may call for an innovation process with phases divided by explicit gates in which higher-level managers evaluate the achievements in the previous phase. A low level of hierarchy, in a flat organization, may call for an independent innovation team that has the mandate and freedom (within boundaries) to create an innovation in close contact with a customer. This context may have a significant effect on the structure of the innovation process. So, from the overarching contextual factor 'organization' a specific aspect is chosen, such as 'the level of hierarchy'. 'The level of hierarchy', in turn, is divided in two values 'low hierarchy' and 'high hierarchy'.

It is important that the aspects that are chosen to represent the contextual factors are specific enough to understand the logic of their effect on the structure, planning, and organization of the innovation process. It is also important to select a limited number of alternative values for each of those aspects to keep the vision of contextual innovation comprehensive yet comprehensible.

For each of the contextual factors, Table 5.1 provides examples of possible aspects and their alternative values. This table reflects the notion that contextual factors are chosen, after which the key aspects to operationalize these factors are selected and the relevant values for each of the aspects are formulated.

Table 5.1 provides aspects for each of the categories of contextual factors. For each of these aspects we provided two values. In practice when the effect of an aspect on the innovation process is complex, it may be

Table 5.1 Contextual Factors, Possible Aspects and Related Alternative Values

Contextual factor	Possible aspects	Alternative values
Type of industry	Degree of turbulence	High/low turbulence
	Degree of regulation	High/low degree of regulation
	Origin of innovation	Science-based/practitioner based
Type of organization	Degree of hierarchy	Hierarchical/flat
	Size of organization	Small/large
	Innovativeness of organization	Innovative leader/follower
Type of technology	Degree of complexity of technology	Low/high
	Protection for technology possible Degree of newness for the industry	IP-protection/open-source Radically new, incrementally new
	Degree of newness for company	Radically new, incrementally new
	Degree of newness for customers	Radically new, incrementally new

useful to distinguish more values. If the size of the organization has a complex relationship with the type of structure of an innovation process, for example, it may be wise to distinguish between small, middle, and large organizations. However, this addition of detail comes at a cost of making the vision more complex.

5.4 Developing the Company's General Contextual Innovation Approach

Developing the company's general contextual innovation approach means that the effect of the context on innovation processes are explored. This is divided in three steps.

Step 3: Creating a Scheme Reflecting the Possible Combinations of Contextual Factors

In those cases where a singular contextual factor is seen as representing the relevant context of the company's innovation processes, this context can be represented by a one-dimensional scheme (or a continuum). If, for example, an organization is active in multiple industries which differ markedly, and the most distinguishing aspect affecting innovation processes is seen as the degree of turbulence in these industries, then the vision of contextual innovation is captured in a continuum where the aspect degree of turbulence is chosen to represent the contextual factor 'type of industry'. If degree of turbulence can be captured in two values, high and low turbulence, then this continuum is divided in two parts:

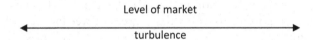

Level of market

turbulence

Figure 5.1 A One-Dimensional Scheme Reflecting the Contextual Innovation Management Vision

In cases where two contextual factors are seen as representing the relevant context of the company's innovation processes, this context is represented by a two-dimensional scheme. If each of the factors, or dimensions, can be characterized by a single aspect with two values, a scheme with four quadrants can be formed to represent the vision on contextual innovation. If, for example, 'industry turbulence' (type of industry) and 'degree of newness for customers' (type of technology) are seen as the most important contextual aspects then four quadrants can be formed.

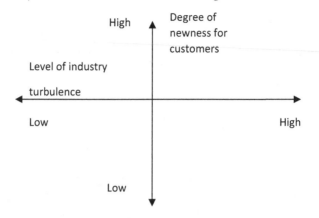

Figure 5.2 A Two-Dimensional Scheme Reflecting the Contextual Innovation Management Vision

In cases with three contextual factors, a three-dimensional system or cube can represent the vision on contextual innovation. In theory, the number of dimensions can be increased further. However, with additional dimensions the number of alternative contexts also increases exponentially, for each of which a specific adapted innovation process needs to be developed. Again, the addition of detail comes at a cost of making the vision more complex.

Step 4: Determining the Degrees of Freedom in Adapting Innovation Processes to the Context

In order to be able to adapt innovation processes it is important to assess in which ways the innovation process can be adapted. Or, to put it differently, it is important to assess the degrees of freedom for adaptation of innovation processes. These aspects will be divided in strategic and operational aspects.

The strategic aspects regarding innovation processes that can be adapted to the context refer to specific decisions that are usually made by senior innovation managers and/or Chief Technology Officers (CTOs). For instance, a decision should be made about to innovate in-house or not. Several options for this decision are possible, such as the innovation processes can be fully delegated or outsourced to a partner, an alliance can be set up, or the innovation process can be fully completed in-house. In addition, the issue should be tackled of how to connect the various, contextualized innovation processes into a larger, overarching innovation program. An innovation process can be part of a larger program consisting of multiple innovation processes or stay or become an independent innovation process. Lastly, the innovation process can be aimed to fulfill a complete set of precise requirements specified upfront, or the requirements are not well-known upfront.

The strategic decisions by top management or R&D managers set the stage for innovation managers. They decide about the operational aspects of innovation, i.e., the specification of innovation processes. Table 5.2 contains examples of such operational aspects.

The second row in Table 5.2, for example, shows several specific decisions regarding the team. A multidisciplinary team seems more logical

Table 5.2 Operational Innovation Process Aspects That Can Be Adapted to the Context

Operational aspects of innovation processes

Process leadership	Process leadership refers to aspects such as: • Type of innovation process leader (e.g., focusing on strictly controlling the process or on creatively facilitating the process). • Supervision of the entire process (e.g., supervisory board for the process, a responsible director, or other authority).
Team characteristics	Team aspects refer to several aspects such as: • Size of the team. • Multi- or monodisciplinary team. • National or international team. • Type of role division in the team.
Stakeholder involvement	This refers to the types of stakeholders and how they are involved, and hence refers to aspects such as: • What are the relevant stakeholders? • In which phases different stakeholders are involved?
Scheduling of the innovation process	Scheduling refers to several aspects, such as: • Explicit phases are distinguished with specific outputs at the end of a phase. • Phases can be completed in parallel or just sequential. • Each phase is evaluated in a go/no go meeting. • The process is specified precisely yet the output of each part of the process is left open.
Flexibility of the innovation process	Flexibility in processes can be changed by considering aspects such as: • Phases can be completed in iterations or sequential. • Subprocesses can be started during the process (spin-offs). • Processes can be stopped half-way if the context or process result is different than expected.
Main information source inspiring the innovation process	The source of inspiration of an innovation process can be regarded as its starting point: • It can start with a technological idea or a patent. • It can start with a specific market or societal need for which a solution (i.e., an innovation) is sought. • It can start with the combination of a new technological insight and a need.

for an innovation that involves both technical and social aspects. A multidisciplinary team in terms of multiple technical disciplines can also be wise if a technical problem is not yet understood and hence the technical discipline that may provide the solution is not yet specified.

All of the operational aspects need to be considered and combined in a consistent way to form a particular innovation management process. A very flexible process with a multidisciplinary team seems an inconsistent combination with a hierarchical leadership style and strict control. What are consistent combinations? In Figure 4.1 (Chapter 4) several ways of innovation management were introduced: technology push, market pull, a combination, networked innovation. These ways of innovation management were described as subsequent dominant innovation management approaches in chapter 1. A technology push approach, for example, would imply that the innovation process is primarily inspired by technological developments, in which phases are scheduled sequentially and in which several stakeholder groups are involved late in the process. 'Technology push' hence refers to a particular combination or operational choices that shape the innovation process. Market pull refers to another consistent combination of operational decisions regarding the innovation process.

Step 5: Designing Specific Innovation Processes for Each Possible Context

This step is the kernel of the contextual innovation management approach because it entails matching the innovation management approach to the context. This is why this step will require a bit more text than the other steps. One of the sources for designing the innovation management approach is the scientific literature. In scientific work the effect of several contextual aspects on the innovation process are explored. Table 5.3 shows a selection of this work.

The first line in Table 5.3 shows how different aspects related to the type of innovation require adaptation in the innovation management approach. The type of innovation, in particular services versus products, are claimed by Hipp and Grupp (2005) to affect innovation processes. Services are different types of innovations and hence a service development process differs from a product development process, and that is having an effect on the structure and type of innovation process.

In this fifth step, it is important to link a wealth of detailed scientific information to the practical knowledge of innovation and R&D managers that are responsible for innovation processes. We advise to form a kind of casebook in organizations to add to the scientific results and explore how separate aspects of the context demand adaptations in the innovation management process (see also Chapter 5). In Table 5.4 we

Table 5.3 Research Exploring the Effect of Contextual Factors on Innovation Processes

Main aspects in the contextual factors	Main results	Examples (references)
Type of technology or innovation - newness to the company, market, technology - new service versus new product	The results show that three types of product newness can be distinguished: new to the market, new to the company, and new to the technology. Each type of newness requires different R&D management practices, for example in terms of the cooperation between R&D and marketing departments. Although service development processes have much in common with product development processes, there are some important differences. Hipp and Grupp state that a different innovation typology is required when services rather than products are described. In his book review of Tidd and Hull, Stahecker writes that "tools and technologies seem to play a much weaker role in services. Another is that the intangibility of many services means that they are relatively more amenable to continuous development than physical goods" (p. 1709).	Jin (2001), Hipp and Grupp (2005), Tidd and Hull (2003)
Type of organization - hierarchical versus flat organization - small/large organization - the firms' competencies, business opportunities, and managerial preferences	The authors describe two completely different sets of companies that develop similar innovations in the same market. Small firms rely more heavily on informal than on formal in-house R&D and use outside sources of knowledge (R&D and licenses) less frequently than larger firms, reflecting their limited capacity to absorb outside knowledge. Above all, small firms depend more on the suppliers of the machinery in which the innovations are embodied. In addition to industrial context, modes of innovation are influenced primarily by a firm's competencies, business opportunities, and managerial preferences (influenced by formal strategies).	Brown and Eisenhardt (1997), Tidd et al. (2001), Miller and Blais (1993)

(Continued)

Table 5.3 (Continued)

Main aspects in the contextual factors	Main results	Examples (references)
Type of industry/ market – high-tech versus low-tech market	Success factors in new product development in high-tech and low-tech markets vary. In high-tech firms, for example, best practices include having manufacturing devote at least 10% of their time to new product development. Low-tech firms had other success factors.	Page (1993),
– consumer versus business market	Business-product companies tend to organize more along cross-functional lines, and they place heavier emphasis on customers as sources of ideas and on finding new uses or markets for their products than consumer-product companies. Consumer-product companies tend to make more use of product management and development groups, focus more on totally new products and line extensions, and emphasize market analysis and product positioning more often than business-product companies.	Nessim et al. (1995)

Table 5.4 Contextual Factors, Alternative Values, and Effects on Innovation Management Approaches

Contextual factor	Alternative values	Suggested effect on innovation management approach
Type of industry	Higher turbulence	More iterative innovation process.
	Higher degree of regulation	More prescribed and fixed innovation process.
	Science based/ practitioner based	Open innovation process or process in alliance.
Type of technology	Newer to industry and company	More time-consuming, risky, and hence iterative pre-competitive innovation process with industry partners, possibly subsidized by government.
	Newer to customers	Closely involve customers to fit the innovation to the daily practice of customers and to fulfill their needs so the learning process of customers will be stimulated.
	Higher complexity	More cooperation with partners during innovation
	More IP-protection	Closer and more secret innovation process until IP is filed and granted.
Type of organization	More hierarchical	More formal approach with gates and evaluations.
	Larger organization	Usually more formal approach.
	More innovative company	More creative and hence iterative process.

re-use parts of Table 4.1 to indicate how this affects the innovation management approach.

Table 5.4 indicates that the context can have a profound effect on innovation processes. In the first row, for example, it is indicated that an innovation process that is to be completed in a highly turbulent type of industry should be structured in a more iterative way. High levels of turbulence mean that during the completion of the project the context (industry conditions) may change so adaptations are required in the type of innovation or the way the project itself is organized. An example might be that a new competitor unexpectedly enters the industry and thereby forces the innovating organization to change the requirements for the innovation that they already started to develop. To adapt to such a turbulent type of industry, it is important to create more iterative and hence agile schedules for innovation projects.

Step 5, designing the innovation management approach for each possible context, can be completed when for all relevant different types of context, the combination of strategic and operational decisions are combined into distinct types of innovation processes. These types of processes are then linked to specific contexts. An example would be an organization, organized in a hierarchical way and in a stable industry. This organization decided (in step 1) that type of technology, in particular incremental versus radically new technology, is the most important contextual factor. The company, because of its hierarchical structure, has a preference for a well-structured and controlled innovation process consisting of phases separated by distinct gates, where management are making a go/no go decision at each gate. So each phase is meant to yield a particular result that can be evaluated by managers before the project proceeds to the next phase. The stable industry also means that similar gates have to be completed for different projects. So, all in all, choosing for a stage-gate process seems a wise decision. However, different versions of this process can be adopted depending on the type of technology (incrementally versus radically new to the organization and its customers). The more radical the technology the more iterative the stage-gate process becomes (because of the uncertain outcome of the project). In the next chapter we will describe how several companies developed their contextual innovation approach.

5.5 Apply the Contextual Innovation Management Approach to a Specific Innovation Process

Application of the contextual innovation management approach requires two last steps (step 6 and 7). For each innovation process it is important to assess the specific type of context. This context should be looked up in the vision to see the proposed guidelines and advices how to adapt the innovation management approach for such a context. These guidelines and advices, in turn, form the starting point informing innovation managers or project leaders how to complete the innovation process for their specific case. We will describe these steps in more detail in the following.

Step 6: Assessing the Values on the Relevant Factors for the Particular Innovation Process

Assessing the values of relevant context factors is an activity that requires involvement of management or customers or any other relevant stakeholder group to agree on the type of technology that will be used, the characteristics of the industry that have to be taken into account during the innovation process, or the type of organization in which the process will be completed.

A radically new technology that solves a problem for a customer of a company yet is not understood by the same customer, for example, may require an iterative or even agile approach of innovation development in which potential customers in a few steps get acquainted with the innovation, its requirements, and how to use it in practice.

Step 7: Selecting the Accompanying Innovation Process

Innovation managers and their team inevitably have to fine-tune and shape the exact innovation process even after taking to heart all the advices and guidelines from the contextual innovation management vision. In fine-tuning the approach several aspects can be taken into account that are not part of the contextual innovation management approach. For example, the scope of an innovation process determines how formal its management needs to be. Once a worldwide corporation is involved in an innovation process, information exchange and discussion need to be organized in an entirely different way than in a small start-up company. Fine-tuning also reveals some of the preferences, competences, and experiences of the innovation manager or project leader and its team members.

5.6 Concluding Remarks

German-born psychologist Kurt Lewin once said that there is nothing as practical as a scientific theory. Although we very much agree with this statement, theories do not become by themselves practical tools. To put theories in action it is necessary to design a process by which the theory can be applied. For the theory of contextual innovation we have designed a process consisting of seven steps that, in line with the theory, starts with the context and ends in contextualized innovation processes. Although the seven steps are straightforward (we hope), we would like to stress that before these seven steps are taken the assumptions of the theory of contextual innovation need to be met. In that sense, the theory of contextual innovation management only has added value to innovating organizations if their 'context' is in line with the assumptions of the theory. Once again, we believe that these seven steps only work if the theoretical assumptions have been fulfilled.

6 Contextual Innovation
Management in Action[1]

Four cases illustrate how contextual innovation works in practice and which added value it can have for organizations. The cases are about different organizations, operating in different industries, and coping with different innovation management problems: making innovation processes more efficient, integrating and combining different approaches to innovation, decreasing the time-to-market, and making product-oriented innovation processes suitable for developing service innovations.

6.1 Case Philips S&B: Making the Fuzzy Front More Efficient[2]

Co-author: Wieger Aarts

The Innovation Problem

The early phase of an innovation process, i.e. the fuzzy front end, is difficult to manage due to its inherent exploratory and uncertain character. The Shaving and Beauty business (S&B) unit of Philips adopted Lean Product Development (LPD) (Ward, 2007; Schulze and Störmer, 2010) to increase the efficiency of the development process. Although it had thereby significantly improved efficiency in the later stages of their product innovation processes, increasing efficiency in the fuzzy front end remained a problem.

In addition, there appeared to be a gap between the innovation processes described in company documents and the actual way of innovating in practice. In particularly, there were alignment problems between the departments and actors active in the innovation planning process (IPP) of Philips S&B, which could be explained by innovation processes that proceeded differently in different situations. Given that at Philips S&B, the IPP activities were to be completed in prescribed amounts of time, the prescribed timeline based on an ideal process apparently could not always be adhered to in practice. For instance, in many cases the completion of the IPP phase differed, taking from eight months up to two years. Changes in the environment of Philips S&B (e.g., changes in the market, economy or consumer demands) could delay the progress of an IPP, requiring a return to the drawing board in the course of an IPP and leading in some cases to unfinished IPPs or changed IPPs. In turn, while monitoring the IPPs, Philips S&B found that the completion of this phase became highly inefficient. It turned out that IPPs were completed in a different order by, for example, omitting certain innovation activities that the innovation manager in question considered unnecessary. The product and innovation managers were not satisfied with the formal, uniform IPP and adapted in practice the prescribed approach as they saw fit, which suggests that a contextual approach could be a better solution. In fact, a kind of contextual approach was already practiced informally by deviating from the official IPP to attempt to minimize the 'political struggle' that would not contribute to a more efficient innovation process.

LPD focuses on the reduction of waste in processes. However, this seems to be in contrast with the necessary exploratory nature of the fuzzy front end of the development process. So, how would it be possible to improve the efficiency of the fuzzy front end without endangering its creative and exploratory nature? The basic idea was that the fuzzy front end looks different in different situations and therefore might require a contextual approach. By making the right choices in the fuzzy front end of an innovation process with regard to what type of innovation process to adopt, the leanness of innovation processes at Philips S&B could be improved.

The Existing Innovation Process

The entire innovation process at Philips S&B, from idea to implementation, was divided into three sub-processes (see Figure 6.1). In the innovation planning process (IPP) (i.e., the fuzzy front end) consumer insights were translated into concepts and product propositions. In the second sub-process, the technology and function creation (TFC), the actual technologies for the concepts and proposed propositions were developed. And in the third sub-process, the integrated product development (IPD), the product was constructed, tested, mass-produced and shipped for the first time. These three sub-processes were technically supported by an integrated architecture (IA).

The IPP was further divided into four activities: IPP analysis (A), IPP insight development (B), IPP proposition development (C), and IPP validation and programming (D). The IPP was described in a work-breakdown structure with major activities and deliverables. For every IPP this structure was used, regardless of the type of innovation and the context it was in. Figure 6.2 illustrates that different inputs were required to carry out these four activities.

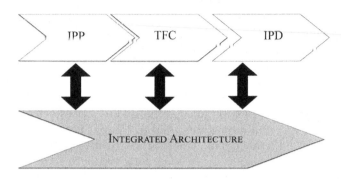

Figure 6.1 The Common Basis of the Innovation Process and the Three Sub-
Processes at Philips S&B

The Contextual Factors

The relevant contextual factors were selected by product and innovation
managers who worked with IPP. They indicated 'degree of newness' and
'driving force' as the most relevant contextual factors.

- Degree of newness: incremental versus radical

Based on the newness of an innovation, broadly speaking two types were
distinguished: incremental innovations and radical innovations. A radical innovation is a new product, service or technology that can provide a
completely new functionality or that can provide the same functionality
based on a new technology. Incremental innovations are modified (or
improved) new products, services or technologies.

- Driving force: technology versus marketing

A market orientation facilitates innovations that offer greater benefits
to mainstream customers and are often based on customer research,
whereas a technology orientation facilitates innovations that apply new
technological principles or new combinations of principles.

The Contextualized Innovation Processes

Three different innovation processes were designed to test the application
of contextual innovation management within Philips S&B. They varied

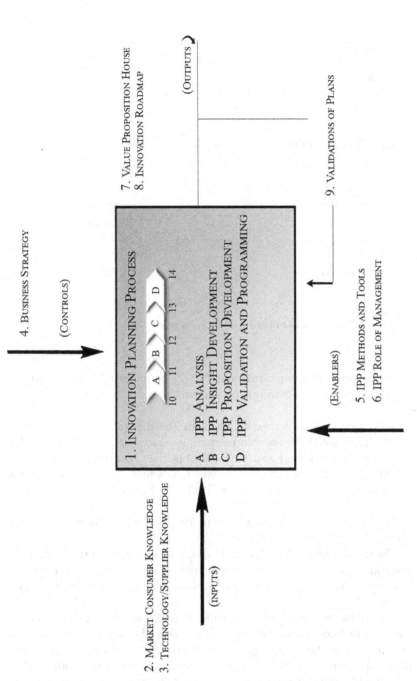

Figure 6.2 The Innovation and Planning Process (IPP) at Philips S&B

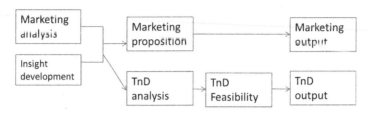

Figure 6.3 The First Option Innovation Process

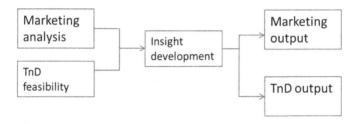

Figure 6.4 The Second Option Innovation Process

in the sequence of sub-processes and in the cooperation between departments at specific points in the innovation process.

> The first option focused on marketing at the start of the innovation process, which meant that marketing created an as clear as possible view on marketing and business objectives, competition, and consumer insights before it communicated its findings to the Technology and Development department (TnD) (see Figure 6.3).

The second option started with marketing and technology development taking place in parallel (see Figure 6.4).

The third option focused on technology development at the start of the innovation process. The aim was to analyze the technological possibilities and feasibility before the exact consumer insights were described (see Figure 6.5).

The innovation processes for eight innovations were categorized by using the two contextual factors that internal and external experts considered most important: the degree of newness, and the driving force behind the innovation. Experts indicated which innovation process-option they would have selected for each individual process and they also assessed whether the two contextual factors and the preference for a specific

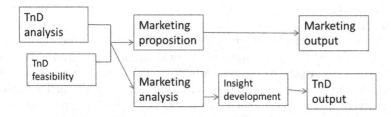

Figure 6.5 The Third Option Innovation Process

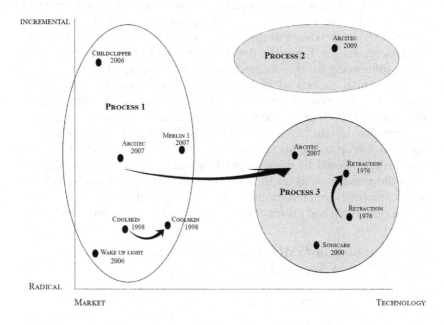

Figure 6.6 The Experts' Opinions About the Most Appropriate Innovation Process for Each Innovation

innovation process coincided. The experts agreed on the positioning of the innovations within the framework. Only three innovations were positioned slightly different by the two groups of experts (Figure 6.6).

Conclusions

This case illustrates how contextual innovation management can be used to develop various innovation processes to make the fuzzy front end of an innovation process leaner (or more efficient). Internal and external experts determined the context of a proposed innovation and chose their preferred process design. The internal and external experts were rather consistent in their opinions regarding the positioning of the cases and the innovation process-options. The positioning of the eight cases by the external experts corresponded largely to the positioning by the internal experts, which indicated that the context of a proposed innovation could be defined quite objectively. The external experts also linked each innovation to the process-option they would prefer for developing this innovation. For most innovations a significant preference for one specific process-option could be distinguished. The preference of external experts for certain process-options differed significantly for different innovations. The preferences of the external experts regarding the process-options for the different cases satisfied the expectations of the link between the contextual factors and the process designs. Especially the factor 'driving force' was an important factor influencing the choices made by the external experts.

The internal experts of Philips S&B concluded on the basis of the results of the case that contextual innovation management contributed to the goals of LPD. It provided them with sufficient theoretical background and practical insight to make better informed choices at the beginning of an innovation process. Because knowing in an early stage which innovation process should be more inspired by market than by technology, or what the ambition level for the innovation process should be (radical versus incremental), will put the innovation managers at Philips S&B directly on the right track and prevent wasting many valuable company resources.

6.2 Case: Boskalis/SMIT: Integrating Different Innovation Approaches

Co-author: Geert de Jong

The Innovation Problem

In 2010, Boskalis, a leading global company operating in the dredging, dry infra, and offshore energy sector, took over SMIT, a service provider in the maritime industry. In addition to the usual problems with takeovers, there arose a problem with the management of innovation processes. Given that before the takeover they had two different, even opposing ways of innovation management, Boskalis and Smit had to decide how to organize the management of their innovation processes. In discussions about the integration after the takeover by Boskalis, the issue came up whether Boskalis' current way of innovating still fit the 'merged' company and its new strategy: could it after the takeover still offer its clients what they need?

The integration of companies is often accompanied by the search for efficiency improvements and other synergies. With regard to innovation, four options were possible in this takeover:

1. The use of one of the two former innovation models in the two companies.
2. A combination of the innovation models in the two companies.
3. No changes, both companies keep on using their own innovation model.
4. Developing a new (different) approach to innovation management (based on scientific literature).

Of course, given the theory put forward in this book, option four was considered the most appropriate. That is, a contextual approach to innovation management could be the best solution for dealing with the different contexts of innovation that arose after the takeover. That leaves the question: by which factors can the different contexts of innovation be distinguished, and how should the innovation process be adapted to each context?

The Existing Innovation Process

Innovation within Boskalis took place predominantly in the Research and Development (R&D) department, which was part of the Dredging Development Department and employed dedicated R&D engineers. In addition, the Central Technical Service Department (CTD) also innovated for tenders and projects that R&D supported if necessary. Innovation by the R&D department was mainly strategy-driven innovation, whereas the CTD was more project-driven innovation.

Incremental innovations, such as efficiency improvement or lifetime extension for a dredging pump, had a high impact on the firm's margins, its competitive advantages, and its competitive position for winning a tender. Incremental innovations also had a high impact because they could be implemented in a big fleet of vessels in numerous projects worldwide, which resulted in the capitalization of economies of scale. The focus on improving process efficiency was driven by the dredging market, which on the one hand was shrinking and on the other hand was showing upcoming competition of low-cost services.

The R&D department generally adopted a closed innovation model. Both strategy-driven innovation as well as project-driven innovation took place. Moreover, both market pull and technology push drove innovation at Boskalis. A stage-gate model was used to funnel down from the idea generation phase to a final innovation phase, where the emphasis was on selection of the most viable ideas to invest in:

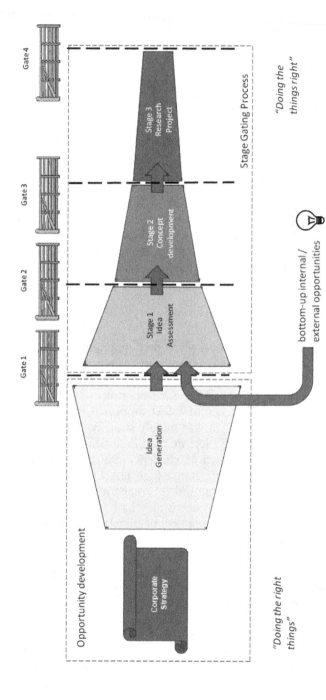

Figure 6.7 The Innovation Process at Boskalis

At SMIT, the role of innovation was to adapt to the changing business environment, continuously meeting changing customer needs, and maintaining the ability to seize business opportunities that stemmed from these changes. Often incremental innovations were developed, when the market asked for certain technologies or expressed certain needs. In these situations, the communication with the client and requirements of the client were essential. Proven technology was often preferred and radically new approaches were hard to establish in this market without a prior project as proof of concept.

However, also radical new structures or new tools were developed that enabled the execution of projects at sea. Therefore, the strategy-driven innovation was important to develop technology separate from the current project requests. This was to be ready for future requests that could be answered with the newest methods. These technology push developments were considered risky and required a vision for the future.

An open innovation model was pursued at SMIT, in which internal clients placed a request for innovation at the engineering department, which in turn looked for partnerships with suppliers and knowledge institutes to achieve the project objective. These partners were involved for their specific knowledge or experience, so that every partner contributed with their core competencies. The use of an open innovation model entailed nondisclosure agreements among partners to protect confidential information. Patents were rarely requested though. The goal of the innovations was to improve operational processes and workability and to develop tools or methods for practical problems within projects. The network in these open innovation projects could be restricted to a few selected partners or, conversely, could be more open to many potential partners, depending on the subject, sensitivity, and goal of the innovation project. The general approach to innovation consisted of four phases:

1. Need identification;
2. Business case development;
3. Innovation project;
4. Knowledge sharing.

To sum up, at Boskalis innovation took place at a dedicated R&D department, at the Offshore Engineering Department, and at the Central Technical Service Department. At the R&D department innovation generally took place in a closed innovation model. Both strategy-driven innovation as well as project-driven innovation occurred. Moreover, both market pull as well as technology push drove innovation. A stage-gate model was typically used to funnel down from the idea generation phase to a final innovation phase, where the emphasis was on selection of the most viable ideas to invest in.

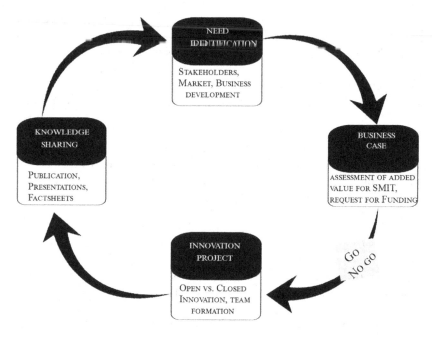

Figure 6.8 The Innovation Process at SMIT

The Offshore Engineering Department of SMIT was exemplary of how it used to innovate in the past. The majority of employees in this department had a SMIT background. Project-driven innovations typically followed the same process as non-innovative engineering projects. SMIT innovated along an open innovation model, although often within a closed network. There were no dedicated innovation engineers, but innovation was a side-activity of the department's engineers. Market pull as well as technology push innovation occurred. And strategic innovation, tactical innovation as well as operational innovation occurred. Project-driven innovation was often intertwined with the engineering process. The frequently occurring tactical innovation often involved the participation in 'Joined Industry Projects'.

The Contextual Factors

The determination of relevant contextual factors for Boskalis and SMIT was based on corporate documents and fifteen interviews with innovation experts at Boskalis and SMIT. Interviewees were presented a list of twelve contextual factors, derived from scientific literature, to which they were asked to allocate twelve points. When the perceived importance of a factor was higher, more points could be assigned to it by interviewees. For instance, the factor 'Level of importance' received +/– 16% of all the points. Figure 6.9 shows the total outcomes of the interviews:

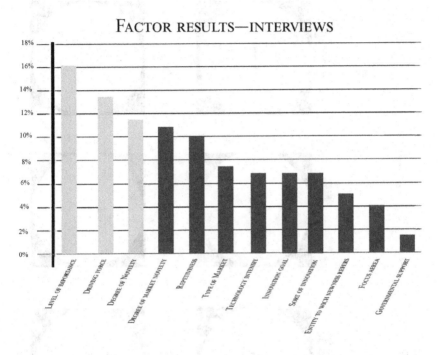

FACTOR RESULTS—INTERVIEWS

Figure 6.9 Ranking by Interviewees of Contextual Factors Based on Importance

Based on Figure 6.9, the following contextual frameworks were established:

The Contextualized Innovation Processes

An analysis of scientific literature on innovation management in combination with expert interviews provided input for customizing the innovation process for several specific contexts, as distinguished in the contextual framework. The aim was to stay as close as possible to innovation models that were currently in use at Boskalis and SMIT to make the implementation of the contextual framework as easy as possible. For the six profiles, five different arrangements of the innovation process

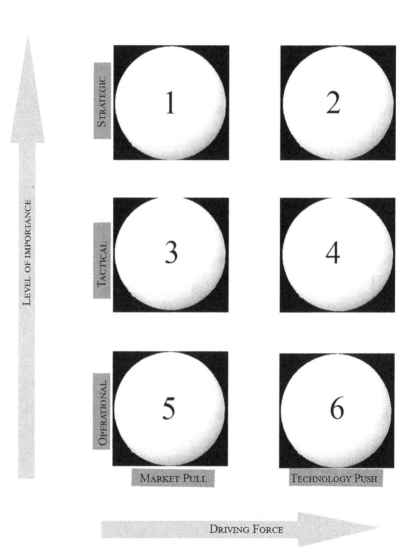

Figure 6.10 The Contextual Framework Matrix With the Six Innovation Profiles

were proposed (innovation profile three and four showed considerable similarities):

Table 6.1 Six Contextualized Innovation Processes

Profile	Strategic Choice	Operational Process	Additions
1	Closed innovation	Stage-gate model	Market Survey
2	Closed innovation Open innovation in a closed network	Stage-gate model	Risk assessment
3 + 4	Open innovation in a closed network	*Joint industry project*	
5	Closed innovation	ISO—quality system engineering process	Multi criteria analysis
6	Closed innovation Open innovation in a closed network	ISO—quality system engineering process	Multi criteria analysis

Conclusions

The contextual framework was tested by two employees of Boskalis who positioned the innovation projects in the framework and checked the spread of the projects over the six innovation profiles.

The current innovation processes and the suggested innovation processes showed several similarities. That is, closed innovation and open innovation in a closed network were prescribed and actually applied. Also, risk management was prescribed and applied in the actual process. In addition, the contextual framework prescribed the use of a stage-gate model, to enhance the right selection of innovative ideas in an early stage of expensive innovation projects and to avoid large unexpected challenges further in the process.

It was concluded that a contextual innovation management framework could be applied as a new approach of innovation after the takeover. It provided alternative choices for the arrangement of the innovation process in different contexts and assisted innovation managers at both Boskalis and SMIT in their innovation-related decision-making processes. Hereby they could fulfill the innovation requirements both efficiently and effectively, i.e., within the shortest time possible and with the least possible resources. This way there was a potential to save resources by eliminating unnecessary activities from the innovation process and a potential to improve quality by emphasizing innovation activities that were important for the specific set of contextual variables of an innovation process.

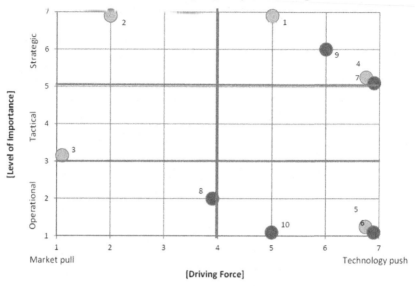

Figure 6.11 The Positioning of the Current Innovation Projects in the Contextual Framework

Origin	Number	Dot Colour	Project
SMIT	1	Yellow	E3 Tug
SMIT	2	Yellow	Polrec-II
SMIT	3	Yellow	T&HL Simulator
SMIT	4	Yellow	Wreck sawing wire improvement
SMIT	5	Yellow	Cable laying concept
BosKalis	6	Blue	Ripper draghead
BosKalis	7	Blue	chatham
BosKalis	8	Blue	Trenchformer
BosKalis	9	Blue	Post-treching
BosKalis	10	Blue	Blockbuster

6.3 Case DSM Food Specialties: Shortening the Time-to-Market

Co-author: Mirjam Fuchs

The Innovation Problem

Time-to-market consists of the time for innovation activities, the time from pre-concept to product launch, and the time required for the implementation of a new product or service. Many companies want to accelerate the time-to-market because that is considered to increase their competitiveness, which makes time-to-market an important strategic weapon.

At DSM Food Specialties (DFS), a business unit of DSM (a global supplier of specialty food enzymes, cultures, bio-preservation solutions, hydrocolloids, savory ingredients, and solutions for sugar reduction), there was a need to decrease the time-to-market of its new products and services. A contextual approach for managing innovation was proposed since it was considered that innovation processes that are customized to their context could accelerate innovation projects and thereby accelerate innovations' time to market. In addition, it was argued that, determined by the set of contextual variables, management could save time by minimizing the resources and efforts on managing factors that are not very important for the specific configuration of the contextual variables of the innovation processes.

The Existing Innovation Process

DFS managed innovation in a structured way, called the 'Business Innovation Engine' (BIE) which was a stage-gate process with five phases, each ending in a formal documented decision:

The Contextual Factors

Several 'categories' of contextual factors (such as type of culture and type of organization) were found in the literature. It was argued that 'contextual categories' such as type of culture and type of industry are 'external' factors and therefore are not relevant in contextual frameworks for single organizations. Indeed, the mainstream innovation process of DSF was already adapted to those external variables. Instead, the relevant contextual factors were related to 'type of innovation', which is an 'internal' contextual category. Based on interviews with innovation managers at DFS, it was concluded that radicalness of innovation was the main relevant contextual factor in DFS. The radicalness, in turn, was determined by two variables: newness of market, and newness of technology

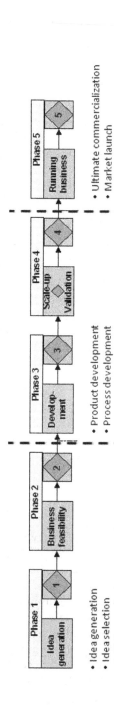

Phase 1

Idea generation

- Idea generation
- Idea selection
- Initial screening
- Pre-concept development
- Concept testing
- Project planning
- Market research
- Decision to make or buy

Phase 2

Business feasibility

Phase 3

Develop-ment

- Product development
- Process development
- Pilot application
- Testing

Phase 4

Scale-up Validation

Phase 5

Running business

- Ultimate commercialization
- Market launch
- Mass production
- Integration in day-to-day business
- Post project review

Figure 6.12 The Stage-Gate Innovation Process (BIE) at DFS

(for DFS). Figure 6.13 gives an overview of the different levels of contextual factors:

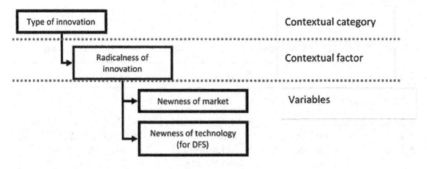

Figure 6.13 Different Levels of Contextual Factors

The Contextualized Innovation Processes

It was concluded that radicalness of innovation was the main contextual factor. And based on the relevant variables that determine the radicalness of innovation in DFS it was found that the innovation process (the BIE) could be customized by using a contextualized innovation framework. Based on interviews, three customized variants of the BIE were proposed within the contextual innovation framework:

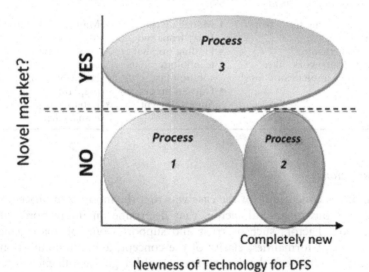

Figure 6.14 The Contextual Innovation Framework for DFS

The three innovation processes were subsequently described in more detail by looking at their characteristics but also at (potential) issues and suggested needs for improvement (see Table 6.2):

Table 6.2 The Three Contextualized Innovation Processes in More Detail

Process 1	*Process 2*	*Process 3*
Characteristics		
• Minimal risks • Full understanding of risks • Full understanding of market and market potential • Fully experienced in technology	• Minimal market risks • Technological uncertainty • Filling knowledge gaps	• Market uncertainty • Commercialization and adaptation hurdles
Issues		
• BIE is too demanding and complex • Too many formalities • Too much paperwork • Decision making takes too long	• Potential of DBC idea box is not fully used	• Lack of market insight • Clarity in product specification • Value proposition • Often unrealistic initial sales criteria
Needs for improvement		
• Managing the fuzzy front end • Less interruption • Basic framework, like: • Decide ◊ implement ◊ finish	• Managing the fuzzy front end • Finding optimal technology solution fast, but: • Current process is quite sufficient	• Managing the fuzzy front end • Effective market research • Extensive market preparation • Extensive risk management

Conclusions

One of the conclusions of the case was that the innovation process was only one out of several factors that determine an innovation's time-to-market. Factors such as trust and support from top management, fulfilment of formalities, clarity of the concept, and communication of goals also influenced the time-to-market, although the influence differed per project. Furthermore, in biotech companies showstoppers such as contamination and scale-up failure can appear anytime and they are difficult to anticipate, because they influence the innovation process's speed very much.

In particular, three conclusions were drawn about the three innovation processes.

1. Innovation process 1 (context: existing market and experience with technology) supported innovation managers to accelerate time-to-market. It reduced time normally spent on decision making, paperwork, and other formalities. Because of a 'final implementation decision' (including the project boundaries) which needs to be approved after phase 2, this process was not only contributing to time-to-market acceleration, it was also suitable for DFS because DFS already had a 'final implementation decision'.

2. Innovation process 2 (context: existing market and no experience with technology) also contributed to acceleration of time-to-market but this largely depended on the success of crowdsourcing in the DSM Biotechnology Center, a supporting unit of DFS. Process two does not only contributed to faster generation of technology solutions but it also stimulated DFS to really start working on the idea or project. Therewith it also helped to reduce the company's risks as one could choose between different proposals and then choose the optimal solution that also simplified decision making. The BIE could be used as usual and crowdsourcing is just an option whenever the situation permits. Therefore, process two could be used without any serious problems for DFS.

3. For innovation process 3 (context: new to the market innovations) the acceleration of time-to-market was not that obvious. It was uncertain if the process directly contributed to a shorter time to market although it simplified decision making (due to extensive risk management) and contributed to the project's clarity (extra focus on product specification). Because of these two factors, it was concluded process 3 was also accelerating time-to-market, however not as much as innovation processes 1 and 2.

6.4 Case Stedin: From Product Innovation to Service Innovation

Co-author: Edwin Oudijn

The Innovation Problem

Just as in many other countries, the Netherlands is going through an 'energy transition' to make the production, storage, distribution, and consumption of energy more sustainable to meet the requirements of the Paris agreement. In addition, the Dutch energy industry is going through changes due to privatization and changing regulations that impact the organizational structure and governance of energy companies. For Stedin Meetbedrijf (Stedin), a Dutch measurement company operating in the energy industry, in particular this meant that it was cut off from its mother company Eneco, a producer and supplier of energy. Another important change is that the energy market is becoming more and more focused on developing and delivering services (i.e., servitization; see Vandermerwe and Rada, 1988).

In the past, the innovation process of Stedin focused on product innovation. However, servitization and increasing competition meant for Stedin that it needed to develop an approach to innovation management that focused on services and for which they attempted to develop a contextual approach to innovation management.

The Existing Innovation Process

Stedin had an innovation process that was formalized in its Quality Management System (QMS) and consisted of five steps, each of which had several sub-steps:

1. Opportunity Identification:

    - Order retrieval
    - Intake forms of new customers
    - Ideas of employees
    - Regulatory change

2. Feasibility study:

    - Global impact analysis
    - Analysis of the commercial aspects
    - Analysis of the technical aspects
    - Go/no go decision management team

3. Product development:

    - Business case
    - Market analysis
    - Product specifications
    - Impact analysis

4. Supplier selection:

    - Assessment quotations
    - Capacity test
    - Proposal of the supplier
    - Purchase

5. Order retrieval

Figure 6.15 shows this innovation process with the order of the five steps:

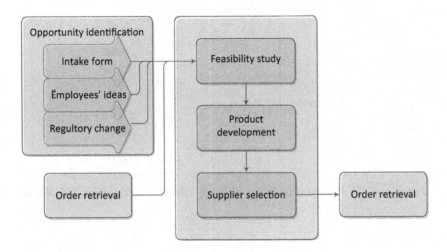

Figure 6.15 The Innovation Process at Stedin

The Contextual Factors

To develop a contextual innovation approach to innovation, employees of Stedin involved with innovation selected contingency factors. In addition, external experts on innovation and with different backgrounds defined suitable innovation processes. The chosen contingency factors were:

- Driving force: market pull and technology push.
- Degree of newness: incremental and radical.

Figure 6.16 shows the resulting framework consisting of four quadrants and the accompanying different innovation processes:

Quadrant 1 (Incremental-Market Pull)

The predominantly mentioned innovation process for quadrant 1 was the 'market pull' process. Here innovations are incremental, so little "ground-breaking" knowledge was needed and that could be acquired via market research. This innovation process can be regarded as the current innovation process of Stedin (see Figure 6.15).

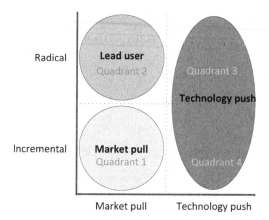

Figure 6.16 The Contextual Innovation Management Framework for Service Innovation

Quadrant 2 (Radical-Market Pull)

The predominantly mentioned innovation process for quadrant 2 was the 'lead user' process because innovations in this quadrant were radical, market pull innovations. Lead users are users that are more involved in new technologies and services and are ahead of the mainstream user.

Quadrant 3 (Radical-Technology Push) and 4 (Incremental-Technology Push)

The predominantly mentioned innovation processes for both quadrant 3 and 4 was a 'technology push' innovation process. Innovations in these quadrants were mainly focused on and inspired by technology.

In Table 6.3, we summarize services that can help organizations to form a suitable innovation process.

Internal experts stated that Stedin develops services in 3 of the 4 quadrants of the framework (see Figure 6.17). The contextual innovation management framework for service innovation prescribed that these services can indeed best be developed with different innovation processes.

The Contextualized Innovation Processes

Figure 6.18 shows the contextualized innovation process in a single scheme. Compared to the current innovation process it adds the demand,

Table 6.3 Services That Were Used to Decide on the Suitable Innovation Processes

Service 1: E-DataPortal:	The e-DataPortal is a web-based portal which presents the measured energy usage of each unit to the customer (Figure 6.16). Consumption can be presented every hour for gas and every quarter for electricity. The e-DataPortal is available for large-scale consumers and consumers with multiple locations (multi-sites). It is not developed for households.
Service 2: E-mail service:	This service provides data of energy consumption in an email. It is possible to receive an email every month, week or even day, with the consumption of one or multiple connections in one file. With this detailed data it is possible to follow consumption.
Service 3: E-History	This service provides historical data of energy consumption to the customer. It is possible to receive historical data for both gas and electricity for 24 months back and dependent on the specific situation of the customer more than 24 months can be presented.
Service 4: E-metering:	E-metering is a web-based portal similar to the e-DataPortal. The difference with the e-DataPortal is that the e-metering provides 'real time' insight in energy consumption. The e-Metering portal is available for all large account users with one or more metering devices (gas and/or electricity) that want live insight in consumption.
Service 5: Dashboard e-DataPortal:	A dashboard for the 'e-DataPortal', that presents all important management info in one overview (not only energy consumption, but among others also CO2-emission and cost). If the 'e-DataPortal' is a book, the 'Dashboard e-DataPortalPlus' is a new cover/page.
Service 6: E-DataPortalPlus:	A new version of the 'e-DataPortal' that makes the 'e-DataPortal' more interesting for a specific group of customers. The 'e-DataPortalPlus' consists of functionalities that are not present in the original portal. If the 'e-DataPortal' is a book, the 'e-DataPortalPlus' is new lines of text on the pages.
Service 7: E-DataBroker	
Service 8: REST server	This service consists of a server that makes raw, unconverted data directly available for customers. With the 'e-DataPortal', data available from the smart meter are converted and presented in a "nice coat" via the 'e-DataPortal' or 'e-metering'. It is also possible to present this data without the coat

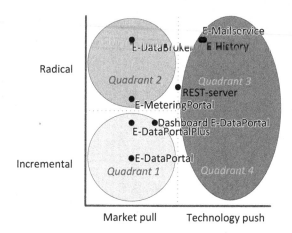

Figure 6.17 Service Innovations by Stedin in the Contextual Innovation
Framework

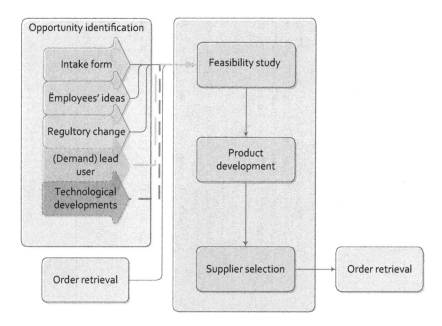

Figure 6.18 The New (Adapted) Innovation Process at Stedin

lead users, and technology developments as potential inspiring starting
points for innovation processes.

The 'market pull', 'lead user' and 'technology push' innovation processes needed to be incorporated in the current innovation process to

contextualize innovation at Stedin. To incorporate this contextual approach for service innovation in the innovation process, Stedin had to adopt changes to the steps in the innovation process. In comparison with the current innovation process:

- Technological developments needed to be analysed.
- Market research was explicitly mentioned before the commercial analysis.
- The demands of the lead user had to be added to the list of sources in the opportunity identification step. Furthermore, the feedback on the performance of the service had to be done in cooperation with the lead user, after the lead user had tested the new service.

Conclusions

The conclusions and implications of the contextual approach for a selection of the innovative services of Stedin are:

- The 'Dashboard of the e-DataPortal' and the 'e-DataPortalPlus' were located in quadrant 1 and could be developed with the market pull innovation process.
- The 'e-DataBroker' was located in quadrant 2 and could be developed in cooperation with a lead user. In addition, the co-creation innovation process, supplier innovation, and market pull innovation process were found suitable.
- Only the innovation process for the 'REST-server' could not directly be deduced from Figure 6.17, because it was located on the border of quadrant 3 and 4. This left Stedin with two options: 1) analyze which of the two processes was most suitable; or 2) try to develop a process that was a combination of the two innovation processes.

6.5 Concluding Remarks

This chapter was to show that contextual innovation is not a theoretical construct but can also be applied in practice. A contextual approach to innovation management is not a goal in itself but a means to reach a certain goal. We have tried to show that using a contextual approach to innovation management can have actual added value to innovating companies. And just as contextual innovation management emphasizes that there are different ways to manage innovation, its added value can also be very diverse. The cases in this chapter illustrate different types of added values.

For instance, at Philips S&B the goal was to make the fuzzy front end more efficient. In itself that is not the most logical goal since fuzzy front ends should predominantly be judged on the basis to what extent creative and diverse ideas for innovation are generated. If that is accompanied by an efficient way of working than that is not a bad thing, but still that is not the most important criterion for the quality of this phase. Nevertheless, it turned out that decisions in this phase can have implications for the rest of the innovation processes. Wrong decisions in this phase, namely, do impact the efficiency of the overall innovation process if the innovation process should be changed significantly in latter phases and the innovation managers have to 'go back' in the innovation process and redo their work. It showed that a contextual approach to the fuzzy front end of the innovation process at Philips S&B, almost paradoxically, by offering more options to deal with the fuzzy front end, made it more effective and thereby more efficient. Contextual innovation management offered innovation managers a wider array of options, thereby helping them making better informed decisions, and subsequently make the fuzzy front end leaner and more efficient. The case of Boskalis and SMIT showed that problems with innovation do not always reside within innovation processes themselves or the chosen approach but can result from changes and decisions in other parts of the organization and in management. Just as with a merger (or a takeover), a decision has to be made about where the (new) head office should be, so do decisions need to be made about the corporate innovation policy. In addition, regarding in which innovation processes to invest money and other resources, the case showed that discussions and decisions are necessary about how to innovate, especially if the existing approaches to innovation are conflicting. Contextual innovation management can then function to ease a potential conflict that can arise from a non-productive debate about which way of innovation management is the best one. After a merger or a takeover, the (new) company will have different business activities and service different markets with different products, services, and technologies. It is precisely this variety that contributes to the possible future success of the new company. Contextual innovation management is very much in line with this variety and can satisfy different departments involved with innovation who have different opinions about how to innovate by providing them with the reason and room to innovate differently and in line with the specific contextual circumstances in which they operate and innovate. Contextual innovation management thereby depoliticizes possible fierce discussions about how and where to innovate.

The DSM case is another case that shows the importance of making the innovation process more efficient, this time by shortening the total time it takes to get from the first idea for an innovation to its actual market implementation. Once again it shows that the most profit can be gained by making better decisions on how and wherein to innovate in the start of the innovation process. It must be said that this case also shows that the quality and added value of the innovation processes are dependent on more factors than just contextual factors (such as support from top management and possible failure of scale-up).

The Stedin case shows that contextual innovation management also can be used to develop a different type of innovation than the company was used to. Increasing the variety of innovation management then supports the broadening of the innovation portfolio.

Overall, from the cases we conclude that:

- Especially in the first phases of the innovation processes, contextual innovation management can have added value. Better decisions based on more variety does not only make the first phase itself better and more efficient, but also prevents problems (and subsequently delays) in the latter phases of the innovation process.
- Contextual innovation management can be an important condition for improving the quality of the process but it is not the only condition. Just as the management of innovation has a context, so does contextual innovation management, which means that other managerial or organizational factors, such as the overall quality of management or the company's overall financial situation, can have an influence on innovation as well. The cases show that both organizational internal and external experts should play a role in figuring out how a contextual approach to innovation can be developed and adopted. Deciding which contextual variables are relevant is a task for both; determining contextual innovation processes (i.e., adding options to the exiting innovation process) is mainly a case for external experts; while testing and checking which innovation should be developed by which innovation process was predominantly done by internal experts.
- Contextual innovation management can make informal ways of innovation management more explicit and thereby legitimize them. That is, in practice, in addition to the official way of innovation management, innovation managers often develop their own style of innovation management since they find out that the singular, official way of innovating does not suit their specific circumstances. Contextual innovation management can then assist them in making their case to higher management that they need a different (i.e., their own) way of managing innovation and gives them the room and tools to do so.
- Although contextual innovation management emphasizes variety, the cases do share certain contextual factors. The distinction between market and technology as driving forces appears in every case and the distinction between incremental and radical is present in two cases. Apparently, these two sets of contextual factors seem to be very relevant and appear in many other studies.

Notes

1 This chapter was based on four master theses on contextual innovation management. The theses were carried out under direct supervision of the authors of this book. The master students have been appointed therefore as co-author for the sections in question. The students are W. Aarts (2010), E. Oudijn (2011), M. Fuchs (2012), and G. de Jong (2013).

2 This case has been published as: van der Duin, P.A., J.R. Ortt and W. Aarts (2013). Contextual innovation management using a stage-gate platform: The case of Philips Shaving and Beauty. *Journal of Product Innovation Management*, Vol.31. No.3, pp. 1–12. The case has also been presented as: van der Duin, P.A., J. R. Ortt, and W. Aarts (2011). Contextual innovation management contributing to lean development: The case of Philips Saving & Beauty. *Euromot Conference*, Tampere, Finland, pp. 430–446.

7 Organizing, Implementing, and Assessing Contextual Innovation Management

7.1 Introduction

Innovation is a process that involves work done by people in organizations. Contextual innovation management is not a process that is isolated from the rest. The essence of contextual innovation management is that it takes the context into account. Contextual innovation processes do not arise automatically and overnight. They must be implemented, which means that both the organization and its people need to fulfill requirements. For example, organizations need to give innovation managers a mandate to determine the right innovation process in the context while innovation managers need to have the experience to do so. And because that does not happen automatically, we cannot assume that contextual innovation management is always properly implemented and leads to the right results. Continuous monitoring and assessment of the contextual innovation management process is therefore needed.

7.2 Organizing Contextual Innovation Management

Contextual innovation management means that the innovation process is adapted to fit the organizational context. Conversely, adoption of contextual innovation management may also require changes in that organization. There are a number of conditions that the organization must meet to make contextual innovation management possible and successful. Here we discuss four conditions:

1. Knowledge and skills: contextual innovation management means that there are several possible ways of innovating. Every way has its own principles, processes, and skills. To properly apply the contextual approach to innovation management, it is important that the organization has the right and sufficient knowledge and expertise. Knowing which method of innovation fits with the specific context of the organization is a first step. This means that organizations need to have knowledge about multiple ways of innovating. To maintain

such knowledge, it is necessary that the organization continues to innovate in different contexts. A highly focused business strategy in which, for example, the organization decides to offer only one product in one market, would take away the need for a contextual approach and on the longer term erode the knowledge and skills.

2. Organizational freedom: Contextual innovation management requires freedom for innovation managers to examine the contextual factors relevant to design, to choose, and to implement the corresponding innovation approaches. This freedom is closely related to the organizational degree of hierarchy. A centrally managed organization will grant less freedom to innovation managers to determine the method of innovation themselves and to adapt this method to the context. Centrally managed organizations may impose a way of 'corporate' innovation management on the entire organization. But it does depend on how specific and concrete this corporate way of innovation management is. If the corporate way is only described in broad terms, for example that cooperation is needed with other organizations, then there are sufficient degrees of freedom for the individual innovation managers (i.e., *how* to work together). It may also be that the corporate innovation management focuses on certain substantive objectives, such as the share of sales of innovations in the total annual sales or the pace of product introductions, and not on what the innovation process should look like. In that case, there is also sufficient organizational room to adapt the innovation process to the context. Implementing contextual innovation management definitely requires top management support (a known success factor, see section 2.2).

3. Innovating the innovation process: organizations that opt for a contextual approach to innovation must free up time and other resources to constantly monitor the quality of the innovation process and to adapt it to new requirements that are set within the context of the organization. Monitoring the innovation process and its outcomes is not new and not reserved for the contextual approach to innovation. But regularly and systematically adjusting the innovation process itself is not something that is too common. But just as the innovations themselves change, the innovation process must change; the method of innovation must also be innovated. It is precisely the essence of contextual innovation management that there is a variety of innovation processes and that those innovation processes are adapted to different and changing contextual conditions. These conditions can change because the context changes over time (and therefore the contextual factors), but conditions can also change when the organization enters a new industry. As mentioned, the contextual approach to innovation arose precisely from the criticism of thinking and acting in success factors that, by definition, are claimed to be universally valid.

4. The formality of the innovation approach: contextual innovation management means that organizations make conscious and formal choices about how they manage their innovation processes. They do this on two levels. First, they decide which ways of innovation management they want to control and apply. Therefore, they have to manage a portfolio of ways of innovating and create the right conditions and organize resources for every way. Second, it must be decided how a certain innovation process should be implemented. A choice must therefore be made from the existing portfolio of ways of innovating. With regard to the first level, it can be assumed that decisions are taken at central organizational level. On the second level, the decisions will be taken much more in consultation between the central level and the people directly involved in the innovation process. There are a number of things to take into account at both levels. For example, it may happen that in the portfolio there are ways of innovating that are diametrically opposed to each other and for which, for example, the required knowledge and skills do not correspond and may even conflict. This in itself is not conducive to the overall efficiency of the innovation policy because knowledge, skills, and resources cannot be used for multiple and different ways of innovating. After all, every organization has to deal with scarcity in resources. Nevertheless, the contextual approach to innovation remains the most ideal method of innovation policy because in that case the overall innovative capacity of the organization is significantly higher than not adopting the contextual approach, thus compensating for possible inefficiencies. In addition, at the second level it is sometimes difficult to accurately determine in advance what the relevant contextual factors are. The specific state of contextual factors such as technology, market, and industry can be determined well in advance, but with a contextual factor such as innovation it is more difficult. In other words, whether an innovation is radical or incremental (two possible values of this contextual factor; see section 5.3) cannot always be determined in advance. Often it only becomes clear afterwards whether it was an incremental or radical innovation, when the innovation has been implemented and has a small or large economic and social impact.

One final note about the formality of innovation and the resulting innovation processes is that the formal nature can be in conflict with the spontaneous and experimental nature of innovation processes. Certainly in view of the trend towards a more 'entrepreneurial' way of innovating, with a growing role for small companies and 'start-ups' at the expense of large R&D institutions and innovation departments of large organizations. Nevertheless, given the importance of innovation, especially for smaller start-up companies, it is important to carefully consider how to innovate because the method of innovation is an important success factor in itself. A good idea for an innovation, a patent or a lot of capital is not always sufficient. There are plenty of examples of start-ups and existing companies that had sufficient access to them but were not innovative. The importance of innovation and the way in which this is done is very important and therefore require a professional approach in which it is clear which choices are made with regard to innovation policy and the method of innovation.

7.3 Implementing Contextual Innovation Management

The previous section dealt with the organizational consequences of contextual innovation management. These consequences are closely related to the factors that play a role in implementing a contextual approach to innovation management. Both the factors and the consequences of contextual innovation management are only relevant and only have an impact if they are actually implemented in organizations. When implementing contextual innovation management, it is important to include the seven steps described in Chapter 5; these steps were also applied in cases presented in Chapter 6. Prior to these seven steps two things need to be explored: 1) a definition of the innovation problem in the organization for which contextual innovation is meant to be a solution; and 2) the assumptions that need to be met in the organization to be able to implement contextual innovation management. Then seven steps to operationalize contextual innovation management can be followed. After these steps, an assessment of the innovation results should be planned in order to constantly monitor and improve the innovation management practices.

In short, all of these notions can be summarized as:

Initial steps to check applicability of contextual innovation management:

    a. Defining the innovation problem in the organization and checking whether or not contextual innovation management can solve or mitigate this problem.

    b. Checking assumptions that need to be met to apply contextual innovation management (See Chapter 4 for these assumptions).

Steps to operationalize contextual innovation management (see Chapter 5 for these steps):

    1. Select the most important contextual factors for innovation processes in the company.

    2. Choosing key aspects and relevant values for each of the selected contextual factors. Formulate alternative values for each of the selected contextual factors that are important for innovation processes in the company.

3. Create a scheme reflecting the possible combinations of values of the contextual factors.
4. Determine the degrees of freedom in adapting innovation processes to the context.
5. Design specific innovation processes for each possible context.
6. Assess the values on the relevant contextual factors for a specific innovation project.
7. Select the accompanying innovation process as a starting point.

Final steps to monitor contextual innovation management:

c. Safeguarding the organizational embeddedness.
d. Assessing contextual innovation management results and adapting and improving the approach.

In the following, we will describe the initial and the final steps in a bit more detail.

Step a. Defining the Innovation Problem in the Organization and Checking Whether or Not Contextual Innovation Management Can Solve or Mitigate This Problem

First, it must be determined what problem the organization has with regard to innovation. Initially, that can be very simple; namely that the organization is not sufficiently innovative. This means that the company has a too-low innovative capacity that manifests itself in, for example, too few innovations, that the pace of innovation is too low, or that there are too few radical innovations being developed. With regard to the latter problem, it is perhaps better to talk about an innovation portfolio that is not in balance. The inadequate innovative capacity of an organization is (subsequently) reflected in a commercial, financial, and economic problem for the organization, such as reaching the wrong customers or insufficiently reaching the right customers, falling sales, or developing innovations that do not have sufficient sales.

In Chapter 6, a number of specific innovation problems were described such as excessively long duration of the innovation process, integrating and combining different approaches to innovation, and extending the type of innovation that needs to be developed from product to service innovation. These specific problems can have their cause in the innovation process itself or in the direct organizational environment of the innovation process.

General and specific problems are interrelated. An innovation process with a running time that is too long can result in a too-late implementation of an innovation and thus cause a low market share because competitors outpace the company. Failure to properly formulate the innovation problem or appoint the wrong innovation problem can lead to the wrong choice of contextual factors and thus to the executing of a wrong contextual innovation process.

Step b. Checking Assumptions That Need to Be Met to Apply Contextual Innovation Management

In Chapter 4, eight assumptions were described that need to be met in organizations and their environment if contextual innovation management is to be applied. In short, these assumptions were:

1. Organizations cannot influence their environment but have to adapt themselves to it and able to do so. (Of course, adaptation is easier to an environment that a company can choose itself).
2. Organizations are able to decide in which environment they want to compete.
3. An organization or its (sub-)departments (or business units) can decide by themselves how to organize their innovation processes.
4. An organizational unit needs to have sufficient degrees of freedom to make their own decisions regarding organizational structure in general and innovation in particular.
5. The context of an organization needs to be sufficiently stable for at least the development time of an innovation.
6. The context of an organization is sufficiently diverse to warrant contextual innovation management.
7. An organization has in its mission 'to be, to stay, or to become innovative', or similar wording, as its core elements. Innovation has to be sufficiently important to an organization to develop its 'own' way of innovating.
8. The success of innovation can be sufficiently specific to be measured.

The subsequent seven steps to operationalize contextual innovation management were described in detail in Chapter 5. After completion of these steps two final steps need to be taken.

Step c. Safeguarding the Organizational Embeddedness

In the previous section it has already been described how the contextual approach to innovation management can be shaped organizationally. This not only concerns the organizational consequences of this approach to innovation, but also how it can and should be organized. Implementing contextual innovation management as intended in this section is more about implementing the contextual approach process, or what steps must be taken to implement contextual innovation management. The organization and the process of contextual innovation management are of course not separate from each other. The organization provides the structure for contextual management of innovation processes and the contextual innovation management process provides, by repeatedly implementing it, a consolidation of this structure. This consolidation is the actual assurance of contextual innovation management that comes on top of the adoption of this approach in the formal corporate innovation policy.

The best guarantee of contextual innovation management is of course the innovation success it generates. Organizations will only choose a contextual approach over a non-contextual one if it significantly and demonstrably improves the innovative capacity compared to the non-contextual approach. This improvement relates both to the comparison with the period when the contextual approach was not used and to competitors who do not innovate contextually. In the (unlikely) event that all competing organizations innovate contextually, contextual innovation management can no longer help achieving a competitive advantage. It would then mainly be about which organization is the first to discover the right contextual factors and the extent to which innovation processes can be adjusted accordingly.

7.4 Introduction

Since assessing the contextualized innovation processes is a rather extensive step and vital to the overall success of contextualized innovation processes, we devote a specific section to it.

Step d. Assessing Contextual Innovation Management Results and Adapting and Improving the Approach

Innovative companies score better on indicators such as market share, profits, and sales than companies that are not innovating or are innovating less. Measuring the innovativeness of an organization is therefore extremely important. There are different ways of measuring innovation in circulation. Dundon (2002) formulated a list of general recommendations that can be used for this purpose and Tidd et al. (2001) developed a list of more specific innovation indicators that therefore can truly be considered an innovation audit. Another example of such an innovation audit is by Gaynor (2002), which contains an impressive amount of twenty-six topics that are divided into four clusters: culture, resources, infrastructure, and process. The innovation audit of Tidd et al. (2001) also consists of four parts that relate to how important from a strategic point of view the organization considers innovation, whether the organization has good external partnerships, whether the organization is capable of implementing innovation processes effectively, and whether the organization supports innovation.

It is important to note that the innovativeness of an organization, and therefore the effectiveness of innovation processes, encompasses more than just measuring the output of innovation processes (i.e., the innovations). It also relates to the quantity of resources that are being put in the innovation process and the way of innovation, so that the measurement of innovation has both a quantitative and a qualitative component. For example, the historically grown broadening of the definition of innovation from 'just' a technical invention to an actual implemented product, service, process, organizational form, business model, and various forms of social and social innovations (Van der Duin et al., 2005) resulted in the broadening of the measurement of innovation (Brouwer et al., 2002). In addition, to develop an adequate picture of the innovativeness of an organization, the measuring and describing of the entire innovation process is important, not only its input and output but also the throughput.[1]

It is not surprising given the proposition in this book that different innovation processes are required depending on the relevant contextual factors of the innovative organization, the measurement of innovation processes is also different. In addition, the innovation indicators used for this therefore differ per type of innovation process. Van der Duin (2006) created an overview of innovation indicators for each phase of the innovation process based on several innovation assessments:

Table 7.1 The Innovation Indicators at the Level of the Organization Placed in the Input, Throughput, and Output Stages of the Innovation Process

1. Input

- Total innovation expenditure.
- Number of persons involved in R&D and/or innovation.
- Number of patents and patent applications.

2. Throughput

- In which broad technological trajectories is the organization active? (science based, scale intensive, information intensive, specialized suppliers or supplier dominated)
- What are the technological competencies and where are they located within the firm?
- How does the organization identify potentially new technological competencies? (corporate visions, technical judgments, product technology matrices, incremental trial, error and learning)
- How are R&D and other innovation expenditures evaluated?
- How are innovation strategy and corporate strategy linked?
- Does the organization use exploratory techniques to identify and predict future trends, e.g, brainstorming, scenario analysis, and Delphi?
- Does the organization seek to develop and maintain networks or formal and informal knowledge?
- Does the organization systematically search for new product opportunities? If so, how?
- Does the organization have a system for selecting (product) innovation in the face or competing alternatives? Is this a formal or informal process?

- Is there a formal procedure for reviewing progress against a series or internship 'gates'? Is this procedure used in practice or are there alternative 'short cuts'?
- Is there top management commitment to and support for innovation?
- Is there a clear shared sense or strategic vision and ownership of the business plan?
- Does the organization have a supportive climate for new ideas—or do people have to leave in order to carry them forward?

3. Output

- Number of innovations introduced over the past three years.
- Percentage of annual turnover due to innovations.
- Part of portfolio that has undergone an incremental change, a radical change, or that remained essentially unchanged.
- Amount of sales or imitative and innovative products and services.

Source: Van der Duin, 2006, p. 58.

The next question is how these indicators relate to the different ways of innovating as the contextual approach to innovation management distinguishes. We conclude that the indicators vary the most in the throughput phase. The input and (especially) the output phase are little to not at all context dependent and therefore not varying based on the way of innovation. For example, the amount of financial resources for each type of (contextual) innovation process will not differ much from each other. However, that does not apply to the input indicator 'number of patents and patent applications' that are more important for a technology-inspired innovation process than for a market-driven innovation process. The number of people involved in R&D and/or innovation, on the other hand, is not that important (although the more, the better for each type of innovation process), but quality can matter. A technologically inspired innovation process will emphasize the use of technically trained R&D staff and the presence of patents. While an innovation process that primarily has market-related contextual factors will appeal more to people with marketing skills.

In addition, the interpretation of the indicators of the output contextual innovation processes will not differ substantially from each other. It is important, however, that given the broad conception of innovation (and that is independent of the type of contextual innovation process), we also look at innovations (i.e., the output of innovation processes) that are not physical and technical. Because incremental and radical are important classifications of innovations, it is also useful to look at the possible social and economic impact of the innovation. However, the degree of the impact of an innovation is not immediately revealed and therefore some patience will have to be exercised before this output indicator can actually be measured.

It does mean that the aforementioned innovation indicators of the output should also measure non-commercial output (such as societal impact).

The throughput phase of the innovation process is therefore the most relevant phase for contextual innovation if one wants to measure innovation processes. In Tables 7.2 through 7.5, we have indicated for the four contextual innovation processes that we specifically consider in this book, which throughput indicators we find relevant. We do this by using the operational aspects of innovation processes as presented in Table 5.2 (Chapter 5) and apply those to these four contextualized innovation processes:

Table 7.2 Innovation Indicators Related to the Technology Push Innovation Process

Technology push	
Process leadership	The innovation process has several leaders, each focusing on their part of the process. There is also one process leader with overall responsibility, especially for combining the different parts of the innovation process.
Team characteristics	Most important qualities of the team are technical skills and the team members should develop their personal expertise. The team is predominantly mono-disciplinary and every member focuses on his or her task.
Stakeholder involvement	Stakeholders are not involved in every phase and those involved must have distinct technical competences.
Scheduling of the innovation process	There are distinct phases and every phase starts when the previous has been carried out.
Flexibility of the innovation process	There is little room for flexibility in the process. Each stage should be carried out as planned in advance.
Main information source inspiring the innovation process	Technological developments are the main or even the only source or starting point of the innovation process.

Table 7.3 Innovation Indicators Related to the Market Pull Innovation Process

Market pull	
Process leadership	The innovation process has several leaders, each focusing on their part of the process. There is also one process leader with overall responsibility, especially for combining the different parts of the innovation process.

Market pull

Team characteristics	Most important qualities of the team are marketing skills and the team members should develop their personal expertise. The team is predominantly mono-disciplinary and every member focuses on his or her task.
Stakeholder involvement	Stakeholders are not involved in every phase and those involved must have distinct marketing competences.
Scheduling of the innovation process	There are distinct phases and every phase starts when the previous has been carried out.
Flexibility of the innovation process	There is little room for flexibility in the process. Each stage should be carried out as planned in advance.
Main information source inspiring the innovation process	Market developments are the main or even the only source or starting point of the innovation process.

Table 7.4 Innovation Indicators Related to the Combined Technology Push and Market Pull Innovation Process

Combining technology push and market pull

Process leadership	The innovation process has several leaders, each focusing on their part of the process. The overall process leader has the special responsibility to combine different parts of the innovation process. Especially in this type of contexualized innovation process supervision is important because there are different innovation processes next to each other, sometimes connected to each other.
Team characteristics	Most important qualities of the team are both technical and marketing skills and the team members should develop their personal expertise. The team is predominantly multidisciplinary and every member is trying to connect with tasks of other team members.
Stakeholder involvement	Stakeholders are not involved in every phase and those involved must have distinct technical and marketing competences.
Scheduling of the innovation process	There are distinct phases and every phase starts when the previous has been carried out.
Flexibility of the innovation process	There is much room for flexibility in the process. The innovation process is an iterative process where stages do not necessarily follow upon each other. The innovation process is not linear.
Main information source inspiring the innovation process	Technological and/or market developments can be sources or starting points of the innovation process.

Table 7.5 Innovation Indicators Related to the Networked Innovation Process

Networked innovation	
Process leadership	The innovation process has several leaders, each focusing on their part of the process. In different parts of the innovation process there are different leaders. For leadership in networked innovation both operating within the process and outside it, is equally important.
Team characteristics	Most important qualities of the team are the skills to cooperate with other people, both within and outside the team and organization. Team members are constantly trying to connect their personal expertise to the expertise from other people and trying to learn from them.
Stakeholder involvement	Stakeholders are heavily involved in every phase and are chosen for the extent they have complementary expertise and are willing to share information and cooperate. Stakeholders are network partners.
Scheduling of the innovation process	Although there are different phases, the process is iterative and is being shared with other innovation partners. The process does not necessarily have to be completed as long as there is sufficient learning taking place.
Flexibility of the innovation process	In line with the scheduling, this networked innovation process is flexible, it is 'open'. Because exchanging information and learning never ends, it is even difficult to point out the beginning and end of an innovation process.
Main information source inspiring the innovation process	In addition to technological and market developments, the ideas and knowledge of stakeholders or innovation partners are the main source or starting point of the innovation process. In addition, during the process new sources of inspiration and information can be used to drive it in a different or new direction or to start a new (networked) innovation process.

As can be noted, there is some overlap between the contextualized innovation process. For instance, both the technology push and the market pull innovation process are linear, whereas both the combination of market pull and technology push and the networked innovation process have an iterative nature. Contextualized innovation processes, therefore, do not differ in all the aspects of the innovation process. We decided not to make the innovation indicators of the various innovation processes quantitative since we think that the throughput phase, to which these indicators predominantly apply, can't be captured in figures or numbers. The indicators should be used as a kind of evaluation background organizations can use to assess their contextualized innovation processes.

Measuring innovation processes assumes that it is possible and even intended to give them a value judgment. The measurement then indicates how the innovation process is doing and what is right and wrong about it. This also assumes a number of absolute criteria on the basis of which the value judgment can be pronounced. It is precisely the contextual approach to innovation that assumes that such an absolute criterion, based on best practices and success factors, does not exist. The value judgment that can be given to a contextual innovation process should therefore always be relative and depend on the specific nature of the contextual innovation process.

The measurement of a contextual innovation process thus becomes both descriptive and prescriptive in nature. Descriptive in the sense that the quality of the innovation process is specifically characterized and quantified on the basis of certain elements. Prescriptive in the sense that the chosen contextual innovation process includes specific elements, as indicated previously. Measuring and evaluating contextual innovation processes based on innovation audits (e.g., the one by Gaynor, 2002) are therefore usually not suitable because they are based on a fixed set of criteria on the basis of which the innovation process is assessed. Making these audits suitable for contextual innovation would therefore mean that a selection must be made from the full set of innovation indicators to allow those to evaluate or measure a contextual innovation process (as was done earlier).

7.5 Concluding Remarks

Changes often start with new ideas. However, thinking differently only leads to doing things differently if it also becomes clear how those ideas can be realized. That also applies to the concept and the theory of contextual innovation management. Just as an idea for an innovation or an invention has no economic impact or social significance before they are implemented, so theories about management only have an impact if they are actually applied. This requires knowledge of organizational conditions that must be met to put the theory into practice. For contextual innovation management it is important that the people involved in the innovation process possess the right skills and knowledge. This means that they control more than one way of innovating. For this, it is then necessary that they are just free to apply multiple ways of innovating, but that they also have the space to learn those extra (new) methodologies. In fact, they must be given the space to innovate the innovation process. This requires that the various ways of innovating are also made formal and explicit. Of course there is always room for "tacit knowledge", since you do not learn everything from a book. However, to identify the different ways of innovating and to acquire ownership, it must be made clear what they are.

If the organizational conditions are met, the next step is to actually implement contextual innovation management. This consists of several consecutive steps in which it must first be made clear which innovation problem should be addressed by contextual innovation management. The steps that follow then focus on searching for and finding the contextual factors, interpreting them and subsequently determining which forms of innovation are involved. This process is not purely an internal matter but must also be shared with external experts in certain areas to obtain the required objectivity.

To prevent contextual innovation management from becoming a one-off exercise, it is important to safeguard it in organizational terms. And for reasons to continue contextual innovation management, it is important to know how it functions and what added value it has. Various so-called innovation audits are available in the literature that offer the possibility to estimate the quality of the innovation process. However, often these innovation audits are based on normative frameworks that indicate how to innovate. In the view of contextual innovation, normative frameworks, certainly if they are unilateral, are not desirable. To have a way of evaluating contextual innovation processes, indicators can be extracted from the various available innovation audits that are relevant to specific contextual innovation processes. This way, every specific contextual innovation process is valued. The results of these evaluations can be used to adjust existing contextual innovation processes or to design new contextual innovation processes.

Note

1 This suggests a linear innovation process that is not intended. Input, throughput, and output can of course follow each other over time, but feedback and feedforward loops are also possible so that the order of the three parts of the innovation process can change.

Epilogue

In this book, we argued that organizations must master and apply different ways of innovation management to ensure that they are successful from an innovation perspective. We also argued that they constantly change this way of innovation to adapt to the new demands that are made from a social, economic, and commercial environment that is constantly changing. This breaks with the notion that there is one successful way of innovation management and that it is of all times. This view argues that in a certain time period, there is one optimal way of innovation that is valid for each organization and for each industry. But that does not do justice to the unruly and varied social and economic reality that cannot be captured in simple and universal principles for innovation. It also turns out that the success factors that describe the optimal way to innovate are often formulated in too general a manner to operationalize them sufficiently precise to apply them concretely in organizations that want to innovate. In practice it shows that different organizations have different ways of innovating which (nevertheless) may all be successful. Finally, successful ways to innovate differ not only between organizations and between branches, but they change also through time which refutes the notion that success factors have eternal value. Different times apparently require different, newer ways of innovating and organizations are happy to adjust their ways of innovation management to the new requirements that are set.

And just as innovations change our society, so do the methods of innovation management. As we described in Chapter 1, the development of innovation management after the Second World War went through four phases:

1. technology/science push;
2. market pull;
3. combination of science/technology push;
4. networked innovation.

This development is evolutionary in nature. Every generation is a change from and an improvement of the previous generation. This improvement is mainly due to the fact that the method of innovation adapts to changing social and economic circumstances. This improvement must therefore be regarded as relative (i.e., temporary). A new generation of innovation management eliminates the disadvantages of the previous generation because that generation no longer does justice to the new demands made by the environment of the organization. The new generation of innovation management does meet the needs of the (new) environment and is therefore automatically an improvement—until the environment changes again and a new and (therefore) 'better' generation of innovation management has to be developed. This change in both the environment of an organization and the method of innovation is characterized as evolutionary, meaning not only that it revolves around change and improvement, but also that the development is gradual. Without starting an extensive discussion about whether social, economic, and technological developments are becoming ever faster and more disruptive, we note that adapting the way of innovating to the new environment of an organization is a process that requires a lot of learning and experimenting. Such a process does not start automatically, takes time, and often goes in fits and starts, where it sooner resembles a gradual (evolutionary) process than a revolutionary process. The generations of innovation management therefore partly overlap.

However, despite the historical development of innovation management with the various generations and the 'best practices' sounding logical and looking gallant, it does not do justice to the way in which organizations actually innovate. The suggested historical development is not correct. The four stages namely suggest that a particular way of innovation is dominant in each phase. In the first generation this may have been the case to a certain extent, but in the later periods there were several ways of innovating alongside each other. Apparently, there is no dominant practice of innovating and every organization chooses and designs a way of innovation management it thinks best suited to their own specific context (environment). This naturally raises the question of how the method of innovation and context are interrelated. The theory of contextual innovation management therefore emphasizes the idiosyncratic nature of innovation and tries to establish the relationships between the environment of an organization and its specific method of innovation.

The historical development of innovation management not only shows the changing manner of innovation, but also the increased importance of innovation for both companies and (national) economies. Being innovative has become synonymous with being successful. It is not without reason that a particularly large amount of scientific and applied research is being conducted into which factors explain the success of companies. After all, if one knows what those factors are then it is only a matter of applying them, and success is assured. Many of these types of research assume that there is one set of unchanging success factors that apply anywhere, anytime. But (unfortunately), that appears not to be the case. Indeed, investigations that lead to this conclusion have either not been properly (or even fraudulently) carried out, or they result in factors that are so general that they are meaningless. Success factors that are valid always and everywhere, are simply non-existent. Often they are only applicable temporarily, or very locally valid. The successful management of a company or economy is therefore an extremely complex matter, whereby new success factors must be constantly sought for.

Despite the persistent and widespread thinking and believing in success factors, there is a theoretical school of management sciences posed by the need to adapt the business to specific conditions: contingency theory. This theory assumes that organizations must adapt to the environment in which they operate. In addition, because environments are constantly changing, organizations must constantly develop new organizational principles and rules. Therefore, laws such as we know in the natural sciences do not apply to the management sciences. The contingency approach is a very interesting source of knowledge and information for the development of forms of innovation management that significantly differ from each other and allow organizations to implement a specific mode of innovation to suit the environment in which they operate.

To adapt the method of innovation to the context in which organizations operate, it is necessary to develop a theory that links the relationship between the various factors of the context and the various components of innovation management to each other in a logical, effective, and practical manner. The theory of contextual innovation management offers an overview of these relationships in which, based on the four generations of innovations, it is indicated how they relate to the different contexts.

To get a clear image of how the theory of contextual innovation management works in practice, it is necessary to describe a number of cases. The four cases in this book (see Chapter 6) are related to different organizations, to different sectors, and to different management problems associated with innovation. The cases show in which different business situations contextual innovation management can operate and what added value it can have for the company in general and for innovation in particular.

Although the cases show how contextual innovation management works in practice, before it is applied by an organization certain conditions need to be fulfilled. That does not mean that contextual innovation management is not suited for every organization. So, the contextual nature of contextual innovation management does not apply for itself. . . . But it does mean that the organizational arrangements should be adjusted to make contextual innovation management possible. And if that is taken care of, the implementation of contextual innovation process can start, which means that certain steps need to be taken to develop a workable contextual framework that enables innovation managers to apply contextual innovation management. Last but not least, the workings and benefits of the contextualized innovation processes need to be monitored and assessed. The organizational embeddedness, a thorough implementation process, and the evaluation of contextual innovation management can make contextual innovation management an ongoing activity for organizations, which undoubtedly contributes to the added value it can have for innovating organizations.

Of course, contextual innovation management is not without limitations and not without criticism. In Chapter 4 we already briefly addressed the criticism on contingency theory, which is the underlying framework for contextual innovation management. But, first if all, applying contextual innovation management can put quite some pressure on the company's resources since being able to manage more than just one way of innovating automatically means that more time and money is involved. Second, employees involved with the management of innovation, but also those who are being confronted with the outputs of innovation processes, might become confused given the diversity of ways of innovation management. Innovating is itself an uncertain and therefore risky process, but if the innovation process itself is also almost constantly changing, then employees might not always be happy with contextual innovation management. Innovation changes the organization by developing new products and services (often for new markets), and contextual innovation management changes the innovation process in organizations. Third, the quality and nature of the innovation process is not the only and decisive factor that explains the success of an innovation process. Often, factors outside the innovation process can be of big influence. Just luck or bad luck can play a role, or one company having more capital available than another company can turn their innovation process into a success and the other innovation process into a failure. In addition, a bad idea for an innovation is impossible to transform into a successful innovation. What we are trying to say that the *management* of an innovation process, whether done contextually or not, does not explain or cater entirely for the ultimate success of an innovation process and of its output (the innovation). We do strongly believe that good management contributes positively to the quality and effectiveness of an innovation process, but not everything in the (business) world can be controlled, steered or managed. We do not believe, however, that innovation is simply a matter of luck (or bad luck) and that employees just have to start working on their innovation without having a goal in their head or without a plan. Recognizing that an innovation process does not equal a project, we do make a distinction between the management of an innovation process and having a purely entrepreneurial attitude toward innovation which basically comes down to taking a lot of risks (almost gambling) and just working harder than your competitors. Innovating is an uncertain process of which a positive outcome can be increased if the way of working within the innovation process and the organizational context is in line with.

The concept and theory of contextual innovation management is meant to change the view on innovation management and the actual management of innovation itself. To prevent becoming postmodern, we expect that this theory will keep changing in the future. Maybe not its fundamental view on the management of innovation as something that is not guided by eternally valid success factors, but contextual factors, the way they influence the practice of innovation management, and the innovation management practices themselves, will not stay constant. Organizations will keep searching for new ways of innovation management and new contextual factors. Scientists, of course, can assist them into this innovation journey, by constantly exploring possible new contextual factors and validating the linkages between those factors and the different possible ways of innovation management. That is why one success factor for the development of the theory of contextual innovation management is the close cooperation between innovating companies and innovation scholars.

In this book, we focused on commercial organizations that try to become or stay innovative by managing their innovation processes. But, non-commercial organizations also innovate, such as governmental organizations (national, regional, and local). Although we did not explore what contextual innovation management could mean to these type of organizations, we do not have reason to accept that it might not be a fruitful concept for them because, just like commercial organizations, they operate in various contexts that change throughout time. In particular, it would be interesting to investigate how the governmental innovation policies (national, regional, and local) would and could relate to companies that have a contextual approach to innovation management. A first hunch is that the variety of innovation policies would mirror the variety of innovation management practices of companies.

References

Aarts, W. (2010). Managing contextual innovation: An expert based case study at Philips shaving & beauty. Master thesis, Delft University of Technology

Abernathy, W.J. (1978). *The productivity dilemma.* Baltimore: John Hopkins University Press

Abernathy, W.J. and K.B. Clark (1985). Innovation: Mapping the winds of creative destruction. *Research Policy*, Vol.14, pp. 3–22

Adams, R., J. Bessant and R. Phelps (2006). Innovation management: A review. *International Journal of Management Reviews*, Vol.8, No.1, pp. 21–47

Adner, R. (2006). Match your innovation strategy to your innovation ecosystem. *Harvard Business Review*, April, pp. 1–9

Amason, A.C. and A.C. Mooney (2008). The Icarus paradox revisited: How strong performance sows the seeds of dysfunction in future strategic decision-making. Strategic Organization, Vol.64, pp. 407–434

Amidon Rogers, D.M. (1996). The challenge of fifth generation R&D. *Research Technology Management*, July–August, pp. 33–41

Astley, W.G. and A.H. van de Ven (1983). Central perspectives on debates in organization theory. *Administrative Science Quarterly*, Vol.28, pp. 245–273

Bacco, F. and P.A. van der Duin (2010). How to apply open innovation in a closed environment. The case of the Dutch defense intelligence and security service. *IAMOT-conference*, March, Cairo, Egypt

Balachandra, R. and J.H. Friar (1997). Factors for success *in R&D projects and new product Innovation: A contextual framework. IEEE Transactions on Engineering Management*, Vol.44, No.3, August, pp. 276–287

Baldwin, C. and E. von Hippel (2011). Modelling a paradigm shift: From producer innovation to user and open collaborative innovation. *Organization Science*, Vol.22, No.6, pp. 1399–1417

Barczak, G., A. Griffin and K.B. Kahn (2009). PERSPECTIVE: Trends and drivers of success in NPD practices: Results of the 2003 PDMA best practices study. *Journal of Product Innovation Management*, Vol.26, No.1, pp. 3–23

Bassala, G. (2001). *The evolution of technology.* Cambridge: Cambridge University Press

Bennett, R.C. and R.G. Cooper (1982). The misuse of marketing: An American tragedy. *Business Horizons*, Vol.25, No.2, pp. 51–61

Benson, J.K. (1977). Organizations: A dialectical view. *Administrative Science Quarterly*, Vol.22, No.1, March, pp. 1–21

Berkhout, A.J. and P.A. van der Duin (2007). New ways of innovation: An application of the cyclic innovation model to the mobile telecom industry. *International Journal of Technology Management*, Vol.40, No.4, pp. 294–309

Bessant, J., R. Lamming, H. Noke and W. Philips (2005). Managing innovation beyond the steady state. *Technovation*, Vol.25, pp. 1366–1376

Bhaskar, R. (1975). *A realist theory of science*. London: Verso

Blindenbach-Driessen, F. and J. van den Ende (2006). Innovation in project-based forms: The context dependency of success factors. *Research Policy*, Vol.35, pp. 545–561

Brown, S.L. and K.M. Eisenhardt (1997). The art of continuous change: Linking complexity theory and time-paced evolution in relentlessly shifting organizations. *Administrative Science Quarterly*, Vol.42, pp. 1–34

Buderi, R. (2000). *Engines of tomorrow*. New York: Simon & Schuster

Burgers, J.H., F.A.J. van den Bosch and H.W. Volberda (2008). Why new business developments projects fail: Coping with the differences of technological versus market knowledge. *Long Range Planning*, Vol.41, pp. 55–73

Burns, T. and G.M. Stalker (1961). *The management of innovation*. London: Tavistock Publication

Bush, V. (1945). *Science the endless frontier: A report to the president by Vannevar Bush. Director of the Office of Scientific Research and Development*. Washington: United States Government Printing Office.

Carlsson, B. et al. (2002). Innovation systems: Analytical and methodological issues. *Research Policy*, Vol.31, pp. 233–245

Channon, D.F. (1973). *The strategy and structure of British enterprises*. London: Macmillan

Chapman, R.L., C.E. O'Mara, S. Ronchi and M. Corso (2001). Continuous product innovation. A comparison of key elements across different contingency sets. *Measuring Business Excellence*, Vol.5, No.3, pp. 16–23

Chesbrough, H.W. (2003). *Open innovation: The new imperative for creating and profiting from new technology*. Boston, MA: Harvard Business School Press

Chiesa, V. (2001). *R&D strategy and organization: Managing technical change in dynamic contexts*. London: Imperial College Press

Collins, J. and J.I. Porras (1994). *Built to last: Successful habits of visionary companies*. London: Random House Business Books

Cooper, R.G. (1994). Perspective: Third-generation new product processes. *Journal of Product Innovation Management*, Vol.11, No.1, pp. 3–14

Cooper, R.G. and E.J. Kleinschmidt (1995). Benchmarking the firm's critical success factors in new product development. *Journal of Product Innovation Management*, Vol.12, pp. 374–391

Cooperrider, D.L., P.F. Sorensen Jr., D. Whitney and T.F. Yaeger (1999). *Appreciative inquiry: Rethinking human organization toward a positive theory of change*. Champaign, IL: Stipes Publishing

Corcoran, E. (1994). The changing role of US corporate research labs. *Research Technology Management*, July–August, pp. 14–20

Damanpour, F. (1991). Organizational innovation: A meta-analysis of effects of determinants and moderators. *Academy of Management Journal*, Vol.34, No.3, pp. 555–590

Damanpour, F. (1996). Organizational complexity and innovation: Developing and testing multiple contingency models. *Management Science*, Vol.42, No.5, May, pp. 693–716

Day, G.S. (1981). Strategic market analysis and definition: An integrated approach. *Strategic Management Journal*, Vol.2, pp. 281–299

De Brentani, U. (1991). Success factors in developing new business services. *European Journal of Marketing*, Vol.25, No.2, pp. 33–59

De Jong, J.P.J. and D.N. den Hartog (2007). How leaders influence employees' innovative behaviour. *European Journal of Innovation Management*, Vol.10, No.1, pp. 41–604

Delery, J.E. and D.H. Doty (1996). Modes of theorizing in strategic human resource management: Tests of universalistic, contingency, and configurational performance predictions. *Academy of Management Journal*, Vol.39, No.4, pp. 802–835

Dill, W.R. (1958). Environment as an influence on managerial autonomy. *Administrative Science Quarterly*, Vol.2, No.4, pp. 409–443

Di Maggio, P. and W.W. Powell (1983). The iron cage revisited: Collective rationality and institutional isomorphism in organizational fields. *American Sociological Review*, Vol.48, pp. 147–160

Donaldson, L. (1987). Strategy and structural adjustment to regain fit and performance: In defence of contingency theory. *Journal of Management Studies*, Vol.42, 1 January, pp. 1–24

Donaldson, L. (1999). The normal science of structural contingency theory, pp. 51–70. In: *Studying organization: Theory and method*. S.R. Clegg and C. Hardy (eds.). London: Sage

Donaldson, L. (2001). *The contingency theory of organizations*. Thousand Oaks: Sage

Doty, D.H. and W.H. Glick (1994). Typologies as a unique form of theory building: Toward improved understanding and modeling. *Academy of Management Review*, Vol.19, No.2, pp. 230–251

Drazin, R. and A. van de Ven (1985). Alternative forms of fit in contingency theory. *Administrative Science Quarterly*, Vol.30, pp. 514–539

Drejer, A. (1996). Frameworks for the Management of Technology: Towards a contingent approach. *Technology Analysis & Strategic Management*, Vol.8, No.1, pp. 9–20

Drejer, A. (2002). Situations for innovation management: Towards a contingency model. *European Journal of Innovation Management*, Vol.5, No.1, pp. 4–17

Dubin, R. (1976). Theory building in applied areas, pp. 17–39. In: *Handbook of industrial and organizational psychology*. M.D. Dunnette (ed.). Chicago: Rand McNally

Dundon, E. (2002). *The seeds of innovation: Cultivating the synergy that fosters new ideas*. New York: Amacom

Echtelt, F.E.A. van, F. Wynstra and A.J. van Weele (2007). Strategic and operational management of supplier involvement in new product development: A contingency perspective. *IEE Transactions on Engineering Management*, Vol.54, No.4, November, pp. 644–661

Emery, F.E. and E.L. Trist (1963). The causal texture of organization environments. *XVII International congress of psychology*. Washington, DC, 20–26 August

Ernst, H. (2002). Success factors of new product development: A review of the empirical literature. *International Journal of Management Reviews*, Vol.4, No.1, pp. 1–40

Evangelista, R. and V. Mastrostefano (2006). Firm size, sectors and countries as sources of variety in innovation. *Economics of Innovation and New Technology*, Vol.15, No.3, April, pp. 247–270

Fagerberg, J. and B. Verspagen (2009). Innovation studies—The emerging structure of a new scientific field. *Research Policy*, Vol.38, pp. 218–233

Farneti, F. and D.W. Young (2008). A contingency approach to managing outsourcing risk in municipalities. *Public Management Review*, Vol.10, No.1, pp. 89–99

Fornell, C. and R.D. Menko (1981). Problem analysis: A consumer based methodology for the discovery of new product ideas. *European Journal of Marketing*, Vol.15, No.5, pp. 61–72

Fry, L.W. and D.A. Smith (1987). Congruence, contingency, and theory building. *Academy of Management Review*, Vol.12, No.1, pp. 117–132

Fuchs, M. (2012). How contextual innovation management influences time to market: A case study at DSM Food Specialties. Master thesis, Delft University of Technology

Gassmann, O. and M. von Zedtwitz (1999a). New concepts and trends in international R&D organization. *Research Policy*, Vol.28, pp. 231–250

Gassmann, O. and M. von Zedtwitz (1999b). Organizing virtual R&D teams: Towards a contingency approach. *Management of Engineering and Technology*, Vol.1, pp. 198–199

Gaynor, G.H. (2002). *Innovation by design: What it takes to keep your company on the cutting edge.* New York: Amacom

Gebhardt, C. (2005). The impact of managerial rationality on the organizational paradigm: Role models in the management of innovation. *Technology Analysis & Strategic Management*, Vol.17, No.1, pp. 21–34

Ghoshal, S. (2005). Bad management theories are destroying good management practices. *Academy of Management Learning & Education*, Vol.4, No.1, pp. 75–91

Godin, B. (2006). The linear model of innovation: The historical construction of an analytical framework. *Science, Technology, & Human Values*, Vol.31, No.6, pp. 639–667

Goffee, R. and G. Jones (2011). *Why should anyone be led by you?* pp. 79–95. In: *On leadership*. Boston, MA: Harvard Business Review

Griffin, A. (1997). PDMA Research on new product development practices: Updating trends and benchmarking best practices. *Journal of Product Innovation Management*, Vol.14, pp. 429–458

Gupta, A.K. and D. Wilemon (1996). Changing patterns in industrial R&D management. *Journal of Product Innovation Management*, Vol.13, pp. 497–511

Hagedoorn, J. and J. Schakenraad (1990). *Leading companies and the structure of strategic alliances in core technologies.* Maastricht: MERIT Working Paper

Halacy, Jr., D.G. (1967). *Science and serendipity: Great discoveries by accident.* Philadelphia: Macrae Smith

Hansen, M.T. and J. Birkinshaw (2007). The innovation value chain. *Harvard Business Review*, June, pp. 2–12

Harrigan, K.R. (1983). Research methodologies for contingency approaches to business strategy. *Academy of Management Review*, Vol.8, No.3, pp. 398–405

Hauser, J.R. and D. Clausing (1988). The house of quality. *Harvard Business Review*, Vol.66, No.3, pp. 63–73

Hipp, C. and H. Grupp (2005). Innovation in the service sector: The demand for service-specific innovation measurement concepts and typologies. *Research Policy*, Vol.34, pp. 517–535

Howells, J. (1990). The location and organisation of research and development: New Horizons. *Research Policy*, Vol.19, pp. 133–146

Hrebiniak, L.G. and W.F. Joyce (1985). Organizational adaptation: Strategic choice and environmental determinism. *Administrative Science Quarterly*, Vol.30, pp. 336–349

Hughes, T.P. (1975). *Changing attitudes toward American technology*. New York: Harper & Row Publishers

Jaffee, D. (2001). *Organization theory: Tension and change*. Singapore: McGraw-Hill International Edition

Jin, Z-Q. (2001). The nature of NPD and role flexibility of R&D/marketing in a fast growing high-tech setting. *R&D Management*, Vol.31, No.3, pp. 275–285

Jin, Z-Q., D.F. Birks and D. Targett (1997). The context and process of effective NPD: A typology. *International Journal of Innovation Management*, Vol.1, No.3, pp. 275–298

Johns, G. (2006). The essential impact of context on organizational behavior. *Academy of Management Review*, Vol.31, No.2, pp. 386–408

Jong, G. de (2013). Setting up a new innovation approach: Applying contextual innovation management to the merger of Boskalis and SMIT in an expert-based case study. Master thesis, Delft University of Technology

Kaldor, N. (1961). Capital accumulation and economic growth, pp. 177–222. In: *The theory of capital*. E.A. Lutz and D.C. Hague (eds.). London: St. Martin's Press

Kalling, T. (2007). The lure of simplicity: Learning perspectives on innovation. *European Journal of Innovation Management*, Vol.10, No.1, pp. 65–89

Keller, R.T. (1994). Technology-information processing fit and the performance of R&D project groups: A test of contingency theory. *Academy of Management Journal*, Vol.37, No.1, pp. 167–179

Khurum, M., S. Fricker and T. Gorschek (2015). The contextual nature of innovation—An empirical investigation of three software intensive products. *Information and Software Technology*, Vol.57, pp. 595–613

Kleinknecht, A., K. van Montfort and E. Brouwer (2002). The non-trivial choice between innovation indicators. *Economics of Innovation and New Technology*, Vol.11, No.2, pp. 109–121

Kok, R.A.W. and W.G. Biemans (2009). Creating a market-oriented product innovation process: A contingency approach. *Technovation*, Vol.29, pp. 517–526

Lawrence, P.R. and J.W. Lorsch (1967). *Organization and environment*. Boston, MA: Harvard Business School Press

Levitt, T. (1960). Marketing myopia. *Harvard Business Review*, July–August, pp. 45–56

Lichtenthaler, E. (2005). The choice of technology intelligence methods in multinationals: Towards a contingency approach. *International Journal of Technology Management*, Vol.32, Nos.3/4, p. 388407

Lieberman, M.B. and D.B. Montgomery (1998). First-mover (dis)advantages: Retrospective and link with the resource-based view. *Strategic Management Journal*, Vol.19, No.12, pp. 1111–1125

Lipsey, R.G., K.I. Carlaw and C.T. Bekar (2005). *Economic transformations: General purpose technologies and long-term economic growth*. Oxford: Oxford University Press

Liyanage, S., P.F. Greenfield and R. Don (1999). Towards a fourth generation R&D management model-research networks in knowledge management. *International Journal of Technology Management*, Vol.18, Nos.3/4, pp. 372–393

Loewe, P., P. Williamson and R.C. Wood (2001). Five styles of strategy innovation and how to use them. *European Management Journal*, Vol.19, No.2, April 1991, pp. 115–125

Lu, L-Y. and T. Chang (2002). A contingency model for studying R&D-marketing integration in NPD context. *International Journal of Technology Management*, Vol.24, Nos.2/3, pp. 143–164

Lynn, G.S. and A.E. Akgün (1998). Innovation strategies under uncertainty: A contingency approach for new product development. *Engineering Management Journal*, Vol.10, No.3, September, pp. 111–117

Maffin, D., A. Thwaite, N. Alderman, P. Braiden and B. Hills (1997). Managing the product development process: Combining best practice with company and project contexts. *Technology Analysis & Strategic Management*, Vol.9, No.1, pp. 53–74

Markham, S.K., S.J. Ward, L. Aiman-Smith and A.I. Kingon (2010). The valley of death as context for role theory in product innovation. *Journal of Product Innovation Management*, Vol.27, No.3, pp. 402–417

Martin, S. (1989). *Industrial economics: Economic analysis and public policy*. New York: Macmillan Publishing Company

McGourty, J., L.A. Tarshis and P. Dominick (1996). Managing innovation: Lessons from world-class organizations. *International Journal of Technology Management*, Vol.11, Nos.3/4, pp. 354–368

Medina, C.C., A.C. Lavado and R.V. Cabrera (2005). Characteristics of innovative companies: A case study of companies in different sectors. *Creativity and Innovation Management*, Vol.14, No.3, pp. 272–287

Miller, D. (1992a). Environmental fit versus internal fit. *Organization Science*, Vol.3, No.2, May, pp. 159–178

Miller, D. (1992b). The Icarus paradox: How exceptional companies bring about their own downfall. *Business Horizons*, January–February, pp. 24–35

Miller, R. and R.A. Blais (1993). Modes of innovation in six industrial sectors. *IEEE Transactions on Engineering Management*, Vol.40, No.3, August, pp. 264–273

Miller, W.L. (2001). Innovation for business growth. *Research Technology Management*, September–October, pp. 26–41

Minderhoud, S. and P. Fraser (2005). Shifting paradigms of product development in fast and dynamic markets. *Reliability Engineering and System Safety*, Vol.88, pp. 127–135

Mir, R. and A. Watson (2000). Strategic management and the philosophy of science: The case for a constructivist methodology. *Strategic Management Journal*, Vol.21, pp. 941–953

Mowery, D. and N. Rosenburg (1979). The influence of market demand upon innovation: A critical review of some recent empirical studies. *Research Policy*, Vol.8, pp. 102–153

Nessim, H., D.J. Ayers, R.E. Ridnour and G.L. Gordon (1995). New product development practices in consumer versus business products organizations. *Journal of Product and Brand Management*, Vol.4, No.1, pp. 33–55

Niosi, J. (1999). Fourth-Generation R&D: From linear models to flexible innovation. *Journal of Business Research*, Vol.45, pp. 111–117

Noble, D.F. (1980). *America by design: Science, technology, and the rise of corporate capitalism*. Oxford: Oxford University Press

North, D.C. (2005). *Understanding the process of economic change*. Oxford and Princeton: Princeton University Press

Ojasolo, J. (2008). Management of innovation networks: A case study of different approaches. *European Journal of Innovation Management*, Vol.11, No.1, pp. 51–86

O'Reilly, C.A. and M. Tushman (2013). Organizational ambidexterity: Past, present and future. *Academy of Management Perspectives*, Rock Center for Corporate Governance at Stanford University Working Paper No. 142, Stanford University Graduate School of Business Research Paper No. 2130; Stanford University Graduate School of Business Research Paper No. 13-1.

Ortt, J.R. (2010). Understanding the pre-diffusion phases: Gaining momentum, pp. 47–80. In: *Managing the diffusion of innovations*. J. Tidd (ed.). London: Imperial College Press

Ortt, J.R. and R. Smits (2006). Innovation management: Different approaches to cope with the same trends. *International Journal of Technology Management*, Vol.34, Nos.3–4, pp. 296–318

Ortt, J.R. and P.A. van der Duin (2008). The evolution of innovation management towards contextual innovation. *European Journal of Innovation Management*, Vol.11, No.4, pp. 522–538

Oudijn, E. (2011). Contextual innovation management: An expert based study into the applicability of contextual innovation management for the service innovation process of Stedin Meetbedrijf. Master thesis, Delft University of Technology

Page, A.L. (1993). Assessing new product development practices and performance: Establishing crucial norms. *Journal of Product Innovation Management*, Vol.10, pp. 273–290

Page, A.L. (1994). Results from PDMA's best practice study: The best practices of high impact new product programs. *The EEI/PDMA conference on new product innovation*

Parrilli, M.D. and H.A. Heras (2016). STI and DUI innovation modes: Scientific-technological and context-specific nuances. *Research Policy*, Vol.45, pp. 747–756

Pasche, M. and M. Magnusson (2011). A contingency-based approach to the use of product platforms and modules in NPD. *The Journal of Product Innovation Management*, Vol.31, No.4, pp. 434–450

Pavitt, K. (1984). Sectoral patterns of technical change: Towards a taxonomy and a theory. *Research Policy*, Vol.13, 6 December, pp. 343–373

Pennings, J.M. (1987). Structural contingency theory: A multivariate test. *Organization Studies*, Vol.8, No.3, pp. 223–240

Pennings, J.M. (1992). Structural contingency theory—A reappraisal. *Research in Organizational Behavior*, Vol.14, pp. 267–309

Peters, T.J. and R.H. Waterman (1982). *In search of excellence: Lessons from America's best-run companies*. London: Harper Collins Business

Pisano, G.P. and R. Verganti (2008). Which kind of collaboration is right for you? *Harvard Business Review*, December, pp. 1–8

Pohlmann, M. (2005). The evolution of innovation: Cultural backgrounds and the use of innovation models. *Technology Analysis & Strategic Management*, Vol.17, No.1, March, pp. 9–19

Prahalad, C.K. and G. Hamel (1994). Strategy as a field of study: Why search for a new paradigm? *Strategic Management Journal*, Vol.15, No.S2, pp. 5–16

Reinmoeller, P. and N. van Baardwijk (2005). The link between diversity and resilience. *MIT Sloan Management Review*, Vol.46, No.4, Summer, pp. 61–65

Rejeb, H.B., L. Morel-Guimarães, V. Boly and N.D.G. Assiélou (2008). Measuring innovation best practices: Improvement of an innovation index integrating threshold and synergy effects. *Technovation*, Vol.29, pp. 838–854

Robinson, W.T. and S. Min (2002). Is the first to market the first to fail? Empirical evidence for industrial goods businesses. *Journal of Marketing Research*, Vol. XXXIX, February, pp. 120–128

Romme, G. (2017). Management as a science-based profession: A grand societal challenge. *Management Research Review*, Vol.40, No.1, pp. 5–9

Rosenberg, N. (1982). *Inside the Black box: Technology and economics*. Cambridge: Cambridge University Press

Rothwell, R. (1994). Towards the fifth-generation innovation process. *International Marketing Review*, Vol.11, No.1, pp. 7–31

Rothwell, R., C. Freeman, A. Horsley, V.T.P. Jervis, A.B. Robertson and J. Townsend (1974). SAPPHO updated—project SAPPHO phase II. *Research Policy*, Vol.3, pp. 258–291

Roussel, P.A., K.M. Saad and T.J. Erickson (1991). *Third generation R&D: Managing the link to corporate strategy*. London: Arthur D. Little

Salaman, G. and J. Storey (2002). Managers' theories about the process of innovation. *Journal of Management Studies*, Vol.39, No.2, pp. 147–165

Salerno, M.S., L.A. de Vasconcelos Gomes, D.O. da Silva, R.B. Bagno and L.T. Uchôa Freitas (2015). Innovation processes: Which process for which project? *Technovation*, Vol.35, pp. 59–70

Schoonhoven, C.B. (1981). Problems with contingency theory: Testing hidden assumptions within the language of contingency 'theory'. *Administrative Science Quarterly*, Vol.26, pp. 349–377

Schulze, A. and T. Störmer (2010). Lean product development—Enabling management factors for waste elimination. *International Journal of Technology Management*, Vol.57, Nos.1–3, pp. 71–91

Scott, G. (2001). Strategic planning for high-tech product development. *Technology Analysis & Strategic Management*, Vol.13, No.3, pp. 343–364

Shenhar, A.J. (2001). One size does not fit all projects: Exploring classical contingency domains. *Management Science*, Vol.47, No.3, March, pp. 394–414

Shepherd, C. and P.K. Ahmed (2000). NPD frameworks: A holistic examination. *European Journal of Innovation Management*, Vol.3, No.3, pp. 160–173

Sissors, J.Z. (1966). What is a Market? *Journal of Marketing*, Vol.30, pp. 17–21

Smits, R. and S. Kuhlmann (2004). The rise of systemic instruments in innovation policy. *International Journal of Foresight and Innovation Policy*, Vol.1, Nos.1/2, pp. 4–32

Souder, W.E. (1988). Managing relations between R&D and marketing in new product development projects. *Journal of Product Innovation Management*, Vol.5, No.1, pp. 6–19

Souitaris, V. (1999). Research on the determinants of technological innovation: A contingency approach. *International Journal of Innovation Management*, Vol.3, No.3, September, pp. 287–305

Souitaris, V. (2000). Application of a sectoral taxonomy to explore contingencies in the theory of determinants of innovation. *ICMIT*, Singapore, pp. 339–345

Szakonyi, R. (1998). Leading R&D: How much progress in 10 years? *Research Technology Management*, November–December, pp. 25–29

Tauber, E.M. (1974). How market research discourages major innovation. *Business Horizons*, Vol.17, No.3, pp. 22–26

Tidd, J. (2001). Innovation management in context: Environment, organization and performance. *International Journal of Management Reviews*, Vol.3, No.3, pp. 169–183

Tidd, J., J. Bessant and K. Pavitt (2001). *Managing innovation: Integrating technological, market and organizational change.* Chichester: Wiley

Tidd, J. and F.M. Hull (ed.) (2003). *Service innovation: Organizational responses to technological opportunities and market imperatives.* London: Imperial College Press

Tidd, J. and B. Thuriaux-Alemán (2016). Innovation management practices: Cross-sectorial adaptation, variation, and effectiveness. *R&D Management*, Vol.46, No.3, pp. 1024–1043

Torkkeli, M., C. Kock and P. Salmi (2009). The "open innovation" paradigm: A contingency perspective. *Journal of Industrial Engineering and Management*, Vol.2, No.1, pp. 176–207

Trott, P. (2002). *Innovation management and new product development*, 2nd edition. Harlow: Prentice Hall

Trott, P. (2008). *Innovation management and new product development*, 4th edition. Harlow: Prentice Hall

Trott, P. and D. Hartmann (2009). Why 'open innovation' is old wine in new bottles. *International Journal of Innovation Management*, Vol.13, No.4, pp. 715–736

Trott, P., L. Hartmann, P.A. van der Duin, V. Scholten and R. Ortt (2016). *Managing technology entrepreneurship and innovation.* Oxford: Routledge

Tushman, M.L. and P. Anderson (1986). Technological discontinuities and organizational environments. *Administrative Science Quarterly*, Vol.31, September, pp. 439–465

Tushman, M.L. and L. Rosenkopf (1992). Organisational determinants of technological change, pp. 311–347. In: *Research in organizational behavior.* B.J. Staw and L.L. Cummings (eds.), Vol.14. Greenwich: JAI Press

Utterback, J.M. and J.W. Brown (1972). Monitoring for technological opportunities. *Business Horizons*, Vol.15, October, pp. 5–15

Van Andel, P. (1992). Serendipity: Expect also the unexpected. *Creativity and Innovation Management*, Vol.1, pp. 20–32

Van de Ven, A.H., D.E. Polley, R. Garud and S. Venkataraman (2008). *The innovation journey*. New York: Oxford University Press

Van de Ven, A.H. and M.S. Poole (1995). Explaining development and change in organizations. *The Academy of Management Review*, Vol.20, No.3, July, pp. 510–540

Van de Woestyne, M., G Devos and H. van den Broeck (2007). A contingency approach to innovation management: A cross-case comparison. *Vlerick Leuven Gent Working Paper Series*, 2007/20, D/2007/6482/26

Van den Elst, J., R. Tol and R. Smits (2006). Innovation in practice: Philips applied technologies. *International Journal of Technology Management*, Vol.34, Nos.3/4, pp. 217–231

Van der Duin, P.A. (2006). *Qualitative futures research for innovation*. Delft: Eburon

Van der Duin, P.A., M. Kleinsmann and R. Valkenburg (2014). Exploring a design driven approach as a way to enable networked innovation: Synthesis and future research. *International Journal of Innovation and Technology Management*, Vol.11, No.1, pp. 1440007

Van der Duin, P.A., J.R. Ortt and W. Aarts (2011). Contextual innovation management contributing to lean development: The case of Philips saving & beauty. *Euromot conference*, Tampere, Finland, pp. 430–446

Van der Duin, P.A., J.R. Ortt and W. Aarts (2013). Contextual innovation management using a stage-gate platform: The case of Philips shaving and beauty. *Journal of Product Innovation Management*, Vol.31, No.3, pp. 1–12

Van der Duin, P.A., J.R. Ortt, L. Hartmann and A.J. Berkhout (2005). Innovation in context. From R&D management to innovation in networks, pp. 227–247. In: *Managing technology and innovation: An introduction*. R. Verburg, J.R. Ortt and W. Dicke (eds.). London and New York: Routledge

Van der Panne, G, A. Kleinknecht and C. van Beers (2003). Success and failure of innovation: A literature review. *International Journal of Innovation Management*, Vol.7, No.3, pp. 1–30

Vandermerwe, S. and J. Rada (1988). Servitization of business: Adding value by adding services. *European Management Journal*, Vol.6, No.4, pp. 314–324

Verloop, J. (2006). The Shell way to innovate. *International Journal of Technology Management*, Vo.34, Nos.3/4, pp. 243–259

Volberda, H.W. (1996). Toward the flexible form: How to remain vital in hypercompetitive environments. *Organization Science*, Vol.7, No.4, pp. 359–374

Ward, A.C. (2007). *Lean product and process development*. Cambridge: The Lean Enterprise Institute

Weick, C.W. and R.V. Jain (2014). Rethinking industrial research, development and innovation in the 21st century. *Technology in Society*, Vol.39, November, pp. 1–7

Weiss, A.R. and P.H. Birnbaum (1989). Technological infrastructure and the implementation of technological strategies. *Management Science*, Vol.35, No.8, August, pp. 1014–1026

Wind, Y.J. and V. Mahajan (1997). Issues and opportunities in new product development: An introduction to the special issue. *Journal of Marketing Research*, Vol.34, February, pp. 1–12

Yakhlef, A. (2005). Immobility of tacit knowledge and the displacement of the locus of innovation. *European Journal of Innovation Management*, Vol.8, No.2, pp. 227–239

Zeithaml, V.A., P. Varadarajan and C.P. Zeithaml (1993). The contingency approach: Its foundations and relevance to theory building and research marketing. *European Journal of Marketing*, Vol.22, No.7, pp. 37–64

Zott, C. and R. Amit (2008). The fit between product market strategy and business model: Implications for firm performance. *Strategic Management Journal*, Vol.29, pp. 1–26

Biographies

Patrick van der Duin (1970) is currently Managing Director of the Netherlands Study Center for Technology Trends. Before that, he was an associate professor of Futures Research and Trendwatching at Fontys Academy for Creative Industries in Tilburg, the Netherlands. He worked as an assistant professor for fifteen years at Delft University of Technology, faculty of Technology, Policy and Management. In 2006, he obtained his PhD on the relationship between futures research and innovation. He began his working career as an applied scientist at KPN Research, the R&D facility of the Dutch telecommunication company. His educational background is macroeconomics at the University of Amsterdam. Patrick is a member of the editorial board of the journals *Futures*, *Foresight*, and the *Journal of Futures Studies*, and is a research fellow at Portsmouth University. His interests are in foresight, innovation management, scenario thinking, and the interplay between technological and social changes.

Roland J. Ortt (1964) is Associate Professor of Technology and Innovation Management at Delft University of Technology, the Netherlands. Before joining the faculty of Technology, Policy and Management, Roland Ortt worked as R&D manager for a telecommunication company. He authored articles in journals like the *Journal of Product Innovation Management*, the *Market Research Society*, and the *International Journal of Technology Management*. His research focuses on development and diffusion of high-tech systems, and on niche strategies to commercialize these systems. Roland is research dean of the European NiTiM network of researchers in innovation and technology management and is member of the board of the ICE-conference, the IAMOT Conference, and of the editorial board of Transactions on Engineering Management. Roland won several best-paper awards.

Index

Note: Page numbers in *italic* indicate a figure and page numbers in **bold** indicate a table or box on the corresponding page.

Printed in the United States
by Baker & Taylor Publisher Services